"If you are looking for a deep-dive
into the essence of the spiritual life,
filled with humor and a good mix
of Eastern and Western wisdom,
written by someone who has walked his talk,
this gem of a book is the one for you."

Swami Asokananda,
President, Integral Yoga Institute, New York

Cover Art: The Unconscious Unwatched Mind

"I have never read a book that offers so much. Padman mixes his own clarity with sage advice from the ages in the spiritual spirit of the sixties. This is the real thing from a brilliant one-time broadcaster who now, at the advanced stages of life, has provided a real guide to happiness. The Beatles said "Money Can't Buy You Love." The thought process of Eastern spiritual psychology and philosophy described in this book, can buy you love, and happiness - if you're willing to pay the price - the price of working at it." *Larry Kane*

Dear reader, I want to tell you more about Larry, we've been friends for over 60 years, and I want to tell you about Larry's karmic relationship to the Beatles. That all starts on page 289.

And, I'd also like to tell you about the Beatles karmic relationship to Eastern spiritual psychology, and philosophy - which is the topic of this book - which through their music, they brought awareness of, to the Western world, beginning in the "flower power" 60s. For insight on that just keep reading..

When something pushes your button, "It's Your Button"

"Since we can't be what we're watching,
when something,
a person, a circumstance,
pushes our button,
it's always our button"

"You cannot find peace by avoiding life."
Virginia Woolf

Namaste to editors,
Fay Savino and Jim Feliciano

Dear reader, we each have many different, yet all the same, "cul-de-sac" personal and business issues that push our buttons.

If we come to see them as "our" buttons, that they have nothing to do with others, we will become determined to find a way - our way - to accept that we cannot be what we are watching, and so that "we push our own buttons!" And whatever we experience, we see, we think about others, we also experience, see, and think about ourselves. Within the walk to that understanding, we will become hungry to ring down the curtain of our habitual button pushing. That is all this book is about.

This book has one purpose, to help us remember; "We are spiritual beings, having a human experience." *Pierre Teilhard de Chardin.*

"State it loud, state it clear,
state it now so all may hear,
This book is dedicated ever so fondly to
Emily Lemer"

© 2024

*Welcome to the Hotel Karma-fornia
"A World Famous 0-star Hotel"

No matter what you've heard you can check out anytime you choose.

Why This Book Was Written

This book was written to help us each, myself as well, find our way, *there is no one way,* don't let anyone tell you there is, of *consciously choosing* to see that when someone pushes our button, it's our button, and that it has nothing at to do with the button pusher, but always, reflects *our own* state of ego-karma mind.

To help us do this, I've collected hundreds of thoughts by people who are recognized as spiritually oriented, most whose names you will probably be familiar with, and written some of my own thoughts as well. These were regular people, living at various times in history, people who, *just like us,* faced *choosing* one way or the other, and so they can help us "invent" our own way of choosing. The title of a great Fleetwood Mac song describes finding this personal choosing process: "Go Your Own Way."

Some of those quoted include: Eckhart Tolle, Mother Theresa, Michael Jackson, Thich Nhat Hanh, Goethe, Holden Caulfield, Swami Asokananda, The Beatles, Dalai Lama, Deepak Chopra, A Course In Miracles, Carl Jung, T.S. Eliot, Helen Keller, Marcus Aurelius, James Baldwin, Bungalow Bill, Al Pacino, C.S. Lewis, Immanuel Kant, Stevie Wonder, Iyanla Vanzant, Swami Satchidananda - the "Woodstock Swami," Dostoevsky, Sartre, Sigmund Freud, Wayne Dyer, Virginia Wolf, Joni Mitchell, J.D. Salinger, Emily Dickinson, Rumi, Michael A. Singer, Rousseau,

Charlotte Erickson, John Keats, Joan Osborne, don Miguel Ruiz, Thoreau, Oprah Winfrey, Amrit Desai, Ralph Waldo Emerson, Maya Angelou, Frank Herbert, Albert Einstein, Elisabeth Kubler-Ross, J.R.R. Tolkien, John Maynard Keynes, Charles Dickens, Marvin Gaye, Harry Potter, Ram Dass, Martin Buber, Kahil Gibran, Emily Dickinson, Guy de Maupassant, Gandhi, Bob Dylan, The Eagles, and Forest Gump.

I did all I could to assure the validity of all the quotes. However, sometimes there were so many versions of them, that it was useless trying to determine the actual quote. So, I used the quote that I felt most closely mirrored "We are spiritual beings, having a human experience," and changing the world, starts with changing ourselves.

As you read the thoughts and quotes in this book, you will see the differences between the only two ways of living life, with or without past karma buttons, and how both direct everyday life decisions. It's up to us to *consciously choose* one or the other.

I've also included some thoughts from my earlier book, the "The Ego Mind Is A Desert," which pointed out that ego mind created an unconscious *"karmic desert thought system based only on the past. B*ecause of cause and effect, the past then *automatically creates our future, so* we are always thinking as if it were the past; since out of habit we *unconsciously* give meaning to everything we see and do through our memories.

This book, continuing that theme, emphasizes the irreconcilable differences between what *I've chosen to call the three mind thought systems:* Ego-Karma Mind Thought System, Spiritual Mind Thought System - *and it's inseparable twin* - Watcher/Chooser Mind Thought System. More on the three mind systems, pages 20-26.

The only way to let go of past button thoughts is by coming face to face with them, and choosing a way to let them go: *By living everyday life at the crossroads: because flowers can't grow in a desert.*

This is not just another spiritual book based on doing things like meditation, yoga, eating organically, going to this or that class, getting a massage, being peaceful, etc., not that we shouldn't do any of those things. It's about earnestly doing our best to live our everyday life as peacefully as possible - not without acknowledging the real difficulty of this effort - supported by Eastern spiritual philosophy - and not by repressing everyday button thoughts, but rather by lovingly welcoming them, accepting them, free from all self-judgement, and both learning, and practicing, how to let them go.

I'm hopeful the thoughts in this book will assist each of you who read them, to find a way to help commit to a "sustained life long process" of correcting your perception of the everyday human drama of "rain and shine," good and bad, winner, loser, button thoughts. And, *in the very process of doing that,* automatically remember, what we have never, and can never forget:

"What the mind is trying to figure out,
the heart already knows."
Emmanuel's Book, Book One.

I've included Emmanuel's quote to emphasize that it's important to undertake this effort with a *heartfelt willingness,* along with a pursued psychological and philosophical understanding, in trying to understand the answer isn't as Bob Dylan sang, "blowin' in the wind," but rather as Beatle songs alerted us all to see, blowin' in the mind.

It's important to say this book doesn't deny or require, the helpfulness that one could gain by working with an Eastern, spiritually based psychotherapist. And that the ideas expressed in this book are not new, estimates of their discovery range between 5000 BC and 300 A.D. but they are my interpretations of those ideas.

This book suggests judiciously discerning the radical differences between the Ego-Karma Thought System, and the Spiritual Mind Thought System, and then *consciously choosing* one road or the other.

"Two roads diverged in a wood, and I,
I took the one less traveled by,
And that has made all the difference."

"Yet knowing how way leads on to way,
I doubted if I should ever come back."
"The Road Not Taken," Robert Frost
Go slowly. Be careful.

The Beatles And A Potential New Spiritual Age

The potential for a new spiritual age began in the 60s, with the Beatles, with Bob Dylan, with two songs.

In a *consciously unplanned moment,* two songs, by the two most influential musical artists of their historical time, brought worldwide undercover awareness to two completely different ways of seeing karmic history. And then it started rolling, like a rolling stone.

The First Song

The first song was Bob Dylan's epic masterpiece, released in 1963, "Blown' In The Wind."

It expressed an understandably, frustrated viewpoint, which inferred submission to the belief that: The worlds ongoing historical issues of war and peace, the peaceful acceptance of each other, no matter color or beliefs, could not be solved, because like our inability to control the wind, they were "blowin in the wind." They were beyond our control.

"How many roads must a man walk down
Before you call him a man?
Yes, and how many times must the cannonballs fly
Before they're forever banned?
Yes, and how many years can some people exist
Before they're allowed to be free?
The answer my friend is blown' in the wind."

The Second Song

The second song, was the *"first song of its kind,"* when Sgt. Karma brought the band to play.

That was because it gave an Eastern spiritual answer to the seemingly unsolvable, perpetually on going global and personal ego-karmic issues that Bob sang about.

Released three years later, in 1966, that song said that, the answer wasn't,

> *"blowin' in the wind,"*
> it was *"blowin' in the mind,"*

the ego-karma mind where it can be seen for what it is.

That song was by the Beatles, written primarily by John, since he sang lead, and as I said, it gave an Eastern spiritual answer as to the only way to resolve the repeating karmic issues Bob's song sang about: seeing them for what they are.

That song was "Rain."

"You said it all but not many had ears, all those years ago"
From George Harrison's song about John, "All Those Years Ago"

Verse 4

"Can you hear me
That when it rains and shines
It's just a state of mind"
From the song "Rain," the Beatles

"Rain" was the first of many, many Beatle songs,
which encouraged many *60s recording artists, many
still today, and many of us, to "Imagine," the answer
never was, and never will be "blowin' in the wind," but
"blowin' in the mind."

*New York Times, March 23, 2024
Peter Townshend on the Who's
1969 rock opera, "Tommy"

Talking to those of us here today, Peter sees "Tommy"
saying, "We prevail ultimately, by turning toward the
light." "I wanted to explain the human condition with
respect to its spiritual potential, which is that we're
deaf, dumb and blind to our spiritual side."

That the Beatles changed music, hair styles, fashion,
the tenor of the times world wide, is fully recognized.
*What isn't fully recognized is the impact of Beatles
music in changing the way we in the Western world
relate to Eastern spirituality.* Things we take for
granted now, yogic practices, Eckart Tolle type books,
etc., were barely a footnote in the West before the
Beatles.

Verse 4

"Can you hear me
That when it rains and shines
It's just a state of mind"
From the song "Rain," the Beatles

"And in the end the love you take
is equal to the love you make"
From the song "The End," Abby Road, the Beatles

Those two quotes summarize the spiritual message of the flower power sixties, of this book, of all Eastern spiritual psychology, of humanities shared longing for peace of mind. They sing to those young then - those young now - those yet to come.

Along with their meeting the Maharishi in 1967, John's lead on songs like "Rain," "Instant Karma," "Across The Universe," and others like "Imagine," along with George's songs such as, "My Sweet Lord," "Heading For The Light," "Piggies," "Writing's On The Wall," While My Guitar Gently Weeps," and Paul's "The End Of The End," "The Fool On The Hill," "Eleanor Rigby," "Let It Be," "Blackbird," and countless others, Beatle songs opened the closed and bolted door to Eastern spiritual thinking in the West.

They opened it to our understanding of what I have chosen to call: The minds three thought systems.

Understanding The Minds 3 Thought Systems

1 - The Button Mind Thought System

2 - The Spiritual Mind Thought System

3 - The Watcher/Chooser Mind Thought System

1 - The Button Mind Thought System

"We are all the product of our lived realities and our collective history." António Guterres, Secretary General, United Nations. New York Times, 10/13/23

What is the Button Mind Thought System? It is both all personal and collective history. It is the *human memory* of 'what we have named' time. See page 12

Ego created karma, the button pushing mind, they are one and the same, a historically learned thought system, filled with "rain and shine" past thoughts. Without ego, there could be no karma.

Like a karmic ice farmer, ego perpetually re-plants happy and sad, "rain and shine," war and peace, thoughts. This is why history repeats itself, it knows of nothing else. Due to everyday life's inevitable ups and downs, this mind system is never peaceful, thus always conflicted, thus alway defensive, thus always in attack mode via cause and effect, unconsciously reinforcing belief in it self with every thought. All conflict, another word for war, begins in the historical ego-karma mind.

So a lasting peace can never exist in our human outer world, without first existing in our human inner world. Everything starts in the mind.

Like the wind in Bob's song, karmic button mind lives a life of its own, taking the world along for the ride. Our spiritual path's purpose regarding this button pushing mind is: To *consciously* remember, what John sang: "It's just a state of mind." This state of ego-karmic mind in Western psychology is called the unconscious. In Eastern psychology, the "karmic bag."

The thoughts in both our personal, and in the world's shared collective karmic bag, all have different button pushing names such as; self-doubt, hate, violence, jealousy, competition, anger, vengeance, stress, guilt, sin, fear, and war. But they are all one and the same: different versions of ego-karma button mind.

No matter the person or situation, to stop things from pushing both our personal, and shared historical/ collective, karmic "rain and shine," buttons, *we first have to find a way to observe them, admit they're ours, and that they have nothing to do with others. In other words; we push all our own karmic buttons.* To help find a method for each of us - one that fits us - so we can *consciously choose* to let go of *all* "rain and shine" thoughts, *because we can't have one kind without the other,* is the purpose of this book. And, we can do it because; button thoughts exist only in *our* karmic mind. In our doing it, *it isn't easy,* we will remember: We cannot be what we are watching.

How did we get our ego-karma button mind thought system? How did we forget Spiritual Mind? There is no answer, since we only think we've forgotten.

2 - The Spiritual Mind Thought System

What is the Spiritual Mind Thought System?

The Spiritual Mind Thought System is free of all "rain and shine" of all historical karma button thoughts of this world, even those of war and peace, *free also of our "learned" concept, time.* On page 12 you can re-read where the Dalai Lama, a nuclear physicist, David Bohm, and Albert Einstein, all agree on this.

The goal of all Eastern spiritual practices is to unite the opposites of karmic personality, expressed primarily in the physical world as bodies, those of Yin and Yang, of male and female. In our physical world male and female appear to be real, to be separated, opposite.

Below, this well known Taoist symbol, is just one way this male/female spiritual unification is expressed. The world's visible and invisible unconscious opposites in time aren't real. Spiritual Mind is *body and button free.* It just Is.

3 - The Watcher/Chooser Mind Thought System

What is the Watcher/Chooser Mind Thought System?

The Watcher/Chooser Mind Thought System is . . . The *inseparable twin, or the memory* of Spiritual Mind.

It has no ego, no buttons, it is free of karma.

It is the place in our mind that remembers we are Spiritual beings having a human experience. We can use this part of our Spiritual Mind, to just observe our thoughts without judging them as good or bad, "rain or shine," to just observe or watch our karma thought system buttons, and *practice choosing* to let them go.

By finding a way to be more aware of the presence of the Watcher/Chooser mind when our karmic buttons are pushed, we can *learn* to let it help us watch, and thus remember: W*e cannot be what we're watching.*

Dear reader, please try thinking about observing your button pushing mind this way: When we watch a movie, no matter what is on the screen, a horrible scene, a beautiful scene, we know it's a movie, and we know we are just watching. So, for example, when there's a gigantic explosion on the screen, we don't just quickly, in a panic, jump out of our chairs, and run screaming for the exits‼

This doesn't mean if something dangerous happens when we're out somewhere, we don't protect ourselves, or, that if we need a doctor, we don't go to one.

But, because when we're in the theater, we know that we're sitting in a chair, we know we're not the movie, we know we're just observing, just watching.

But, and here's the catch, if something in the movie . . . REMEMBER, THERE ARE NO LIVING PEOPLE ON THE SCREEN: WE ARE WATCHING PROJECTED IMAGES ON SOMETHING MADE OF HIGH GRADE PAPER. BUT IF SOME SCENE ON THE SCREEN pushes our button, and we identify with, or interpret those images *as being real,* we will respond to them.

We will laugh or cry, maybe scream, depending on our accumulated karma buttons. *Significantly,* the person sitting next to us, may have a completely different response to the same scene, because they do not have the same past karma buttons we do. This is an example of understanding that all the worlds differences of opinion on things, for example like, who started a war, or which really is the "best" picture, are *based on one's past ego-karma thoughts. And like watching the movie, we give them their meaning. They have no meaning other than that which we give them.*

In this same exact way, we give meaning to "our daily life" interactions with others, *regardless of the people involved,* on the screen we have come to believe is the world. And just like the movie, they have no meaning, "rain or shine," other than what we give them.

So even though we cannot be what we are watching, just like in the movies, we can get pulled in, in effect: *make an unconscious choice,* to let our buttons get pushed, and forget we are just watching.

Since the Watcher/Chooser knows it is not our past karma thoughts, it can help us choose how we want to respond to any button that is pushed. And, there are only two choices, we can choose to respond with the past, the ego-karma mind, or with Spiritual Mind.

The Watcher/Chooser is the part of the mind that knows we can't be what we're watching. The more we turn to it, the more it functions like an automatic pilot, it helps us establish a continuous *habit* of remembering our Spiritual Mind. In *the process itself* of choosing to remember it's impossible to be what you are watching, we gradually can over time, become free of buttons.

So as said, no matter the relationship; with someone we know, someone we hardly know, with someone we care for, someone we don't like, some one we just "accidentally" bump into in a supermarket, (there are no accidents) or someone we hope we never see again, (:-) we can choose to watch them in one of two ways: With or without *our* ego-karma buttons.

"I'm just sitting here watching the wheels go round and round, I really love to watch them roll. No longer riding on the merry-go-round, I just had to let it go, I just had to let it go, I just had to let it go."

"Watching The Wheels," John Lennon - Wille Nelson and Sons

J.D. Salinger had named his Watcher/Chooser Mind, "The Catcher in the Rye." *(Page 224/25 paperback edition)*

> When something pressed Holden Caulfield's buttons, Holden explained his way of observing and choosing.

> "Anyway, I just keep picturing all these little kids playing some game in this big field of rye and all. Thousands of the little kids, and nobody's around - nobody big, I mean - except me. And I'm standing on the edge of some crazy cliff. What I have to do, I have to catch everybody if they start to go over the cliff - I mean if they're running and they don't look where they're going I have to come out from somewhere and catch them. That's all I'd do all day. I'd just be the catcher in the rye and all. I know it's crazy, but that's the only thing I'd really like to be. I know it's crazy."

If we cannot find a process - *one that fits us* - to *consciously choose* to see differently, we will live, we will experience, we will choose, everything that happens to us now, all decisions we make about our present life, as if we were still living in the past.

So all depends on finding a process, joined with a heartfelt willingness, and a *"consciously chosen"* effort, to wrap our minds around the unquestioned conviction that: We have no buttons, except the ones *we have unconsciously, karmicly, chosen in the past.*

Relationships And The Karmic Buttons,

- Four Spiritual Mind Choosing Principles -

The following four principles can be used with all relationships, including those buttons and beaus ego-karma mind gives favored status to: Parents, children, husbands, wives, uncles, cousins, friends, all relatives.

One. We never see others as they are, but only with our Button or Spiritual Mind, so, there are no others.

Two. To choose to experience so called others with ego-karma buttons, is to deny we see them as they are - now. We will see them as we want them to be, were, but, never as they are - now. They are the versions of them that *we have created in our own past karmic mind memory about them.* And we will see, treat, and talk both with them, *and ourselves,* in that way.

Three. You can't be what you're watching, it's impossible. You cannot be the movie on the screen. *But karma fools you,* and make you think you can.

Four. There are only two ways we can *choose* to resolve whatever happens to us: With button karma mind or Spiritual Mind. with peace of mind or without. To choose one is to abandon the other.

How To Use This Book

Beethoven proved you don't need ears to hear.
Stevie Wonder proved you don't need eyes to see.
There are sounds beyond what physical ears can hear.
There are colors beyond what physical eyes can see.

These first 25 pages should be referred to as needed.
But from page 25 onward, this book can be read page
by page, and/or carried around like a "small friend." In
that way you can randomly turn to any page, and use
any thought you find, "rain or shine," and *any personal
thoughts you have they bring up,* and - don't judge
them - *just watch. Watch* what feelings, what thoughts
they bring up of your lifetime ego-karma collection.

By just watching, in a sort of disinterested, *yet very
consciously* aware, it will help you/us *learn* to make a
conscious effort to find a way, a method, to *choose to
experience our everyday practical life experiences,*
with either the Ego-Karma Button Mind System, or the
Spiritual Mind System as described on pages 15-22.

- The Unwatched Mind -
The Mind Of Time-Ego-Karma-History

As you watch your thought collection, consider you're watching the karma storage bin in your mind that holds the lifetime accumulation of your past thoughts. You're watching the "person-ality you've *taught* yourself to become. You're watching what normally in everyday life is unwatched, but is referred to for all decisions.

But we should learn to watch it, just like we watch movies or videos, because this is the only way we can choose how we want to experience our daily life, the only way we can gradually prevent this place in our mind, from choosing for is how we live our life. And there are only two mind choices: Forms of conflict, doubt, fear, stress, anger, etc., or peace of mind.

Psychology has named this unwatched mind "the unconscious." I suggest this mind which has and continues to be, the source of all known universal physical form, and all human creativity, both good and bad, should no longer naïvely and incorrectly referred to as "unconscious," but rather as **unwatched** because it is a consciousness of a kind, and must be seen for what it is: A mind created by *non-existent time, with a name it has given itself: Ego. And this ego identity then created a corresponding, unified thought system to represent it: *Time-History-Karma. *Page's 28-31.

From the mistaken belief we are ego-karma beings, we have deceived ourselves in creating this thought system. Eastern spirituality systems call it the illusion. Understanding its emptiness, it is in a continuous state of fear and conflict. A look back at conflicted world history between nations and people verifies this idea. No longer must it be seen as ~~unconscious,~~ but as unwatched. And then watched and seen for what it is.

The benefit of learning, of finding a way to watch this mind, from which we give meaning to everything we experience is, it frees us to **chose** how we want to experience our life, with peace of mind, or without. The benefit of finding and practicing a process to accomplish this is easily explained by considering why a surgeon never operates on their own family.

Watching the Unwatched Mind:
Choosing How We Would Live Our Life"

And so dear reader, as you read the thoughts on the following pages, be aware of the past thoughts and feelings they bring to your mind. But no matter what comes, gently try to be non-judgmental towards them, not to judge them as good or bad, but rather as they're coming up to be seen, seen lovingly, non-judgmentally, like a loving parent sees a child, with Spiritual Mind.

And keep in mind as you practice watching, with each choice you remember with more certainty, *choose* with more certainty, how you would experience your life: with Button Mind, or Spiritual Mind, regardless of outside circumstances, but without denying outside circumstances. We can't avoid our karma.

Over time you'll watch without even thinking about it, because like any habit, the habit of watching will just take over. Our shared spiritual life is a story *waiting to be chosen. A*nd there are only two choices.

You are not your thoughts, because you/we can't be what we're watching. P*ractice learning* to watch, just like you're watching a movie or a video, or a game.

You already are the Watcher. Belief in ego mind; in time, in karma, in history, in the past, in the movie, has made you/us think we've forgotten. We practice to remember. Namaste to you in all you do dear reader.

The Mind Of Time

Have you ever taken a breath when it wasn't now? The Dalai Lama, a quantum physicist, David Bohm,

Einstein's theory of relativity, and Marcus Aurelius, each explain why Eastern spiritual psychology, Eckert Tolle, A Course In Miracles, Yogic teachings, and all Eastern spiritual teachings, say: The only time is now.

"The more you are focused on time, past and future, the more you miss the Now. Make the NOW, the primary focus of your life." *Eckhart Tolle*

"Take this very instant, now, and think of it as all there is of time." *A Course In Miracles*

"Remember that man lives only in the present, in this fleeting instant; all the rest of his life is either past and gone, or not yet revealed." *Marcus Aurelius*

Commenting on "Einstein's Theory Of Relativity, below is a paraphrased quote by the Dalai Lama regarding time, from page 59 of his book, "The Universe In A Single Atom," and so our perception of time, birth, death, and thus, our pushed karmic buttons. *"There's no real time that has an existence of its own."*

Time is a button pushing effect of karma mind.

Karma's Purpose

Being nothing, does time-karma have a purpose? Yes.
Time-karma's purpose is to help us remember: "We're
spiritual beings having a human experience." There
will never be another karma-time to remember this,
than what seems to be now.

Karma Is Like A River Without Water

Karma is like a river without water,
like a motherless daughter,
like an ocean with no shore in sight,
like a song always playing backwards.

Karma is like a sold out sell out,
Always trying to find out more about
Where it's never been.
Karma is like Yang without Yin.

Karma is like a person without a name,
like a melody without a song,
like a winter storm in the middle of June.
Time is like a Beatle song without a tune.
Karma is like a river without water

Karma is time.

"Time is the space between the observer and the tree."
Krishnamurti

Time is history.

Nothing New Happens In History

"Sooner or later it'll be found,
nothing new happens in history." *Carl Jung*

Dear reader, I first heard about an Eastern spiritual
approach to everyday life by listening to songs by the
Beatles, more on this on page 16, and other artists who
picked up on it, "All Those Years Ago" in the 60's.

That time was a historical moment similar to this one,
a tumultuous decade: Assassinations, demonstrations,
shootings, racial issues, life and hair style changes, a
foreign war, and drug use. It was a time of another
warring Russian leader, a time when people were
fleeing one country to go to another. There were riots
in our cities, and threats of nuclear destruction … back
then they were just 485 miles from the Florida shore.
I'm sure you can see, karmically, it was a decade that
resembles - in many of the same, yet different ways -
the one we're living now. Life Magazine called it;
"The Decade of Tumult and Change."

I don't want to go on and on about all that. Those of us
who were there back then know it all, those of us still
left here, *based on lived experience,* can see, as Jung
said, *"*nothing new happens in history," humankind's
karmic errors keep repeating, albeit in different forms,
because: We're using the button pushing karmic mind
set that created all the problems, to try to solve them.
And so, *unconsciously* causing history to repeat itself.

What Is History?

"History is new people making old mistakes."
Sigmund Freud

History is: Human caused ego-karma. Karma is like a river without water. Karma is learned *unconscious* ego *button mind sets of the past.* Knowing nothing but its own past thoughts of karmic time, of humanities shared ego-history mind, karmic button mind can only make decisions about what it does now, based on what it knows, and all it knows is the past. So as I said, humanity is using the very same mind set that created "Decades of Tumult and Change," those tumultuous karmic winds of past history, to undo what *it* did.

In this way ego mind - cleverly disguises itself as some new solution, some new law, some new peace treaty, to resolve the problems *it* has caused in the past, using the same boomerang mind that created the problems!

This tricks us to, frustratingly, mistakenly, repeatedly proclaim, as Bob Dylans 60s masterpiece did:
"the answer is blowin' in the wind"

Western psychological inner value thought systems, and their concurrent outer value thought systems, do not represent all world consciousness and value systems. They represent a particular accumulated educational, historical, acculturated, value system, defining a particular segment of mankind.

Ego-karma invented J. Robert Oppenheimer, and, well; you know the rest.

"I saw a film today, oh boy

The English Army had just won the war"
From the Beatles song "A Day In The Life"

If Marlon Brando played the Godfather, all day, every day, for 20 years, Marlon Brando would forget who Marlon Brando was. Can you hear me?

You can see all others, no exceptions, with or without buttons.

Birth begins button activation days. We don't have any buttons, but the ego, that is, the person we think we are, has convinced us we do.

As you push your buttons, so you become. As you un-push your buttons, so you become.

The ego is afraid of its own shadow, not recognizing, it is its own shadow.

To become totally button free is the only goal of Eastern spiritual psychology. The only way to become totally button free is to practice, to practice recalling that we already are.

Ego recycles everything, calls it karma.

STRESS

"Fear is the mind killer." *Frank Herbert, "Dune"*

A few words about stress, I say a few, because just reading the word itself - because we've become so identified with it - whether we consciously notice it or not, causes us to become "stressed."

We must however, accept that it is nearly impossible to go through our everyday lives, with all its up's and downs, it's good and bad's, and not experience some form of stress, because: *Stress is accumulated karma.*

It's crucial to understand that stress is of form of karma, because if we had nothing to fear, nothing to worry about, no karma, we would have no stress. Eastern, spiritual, psychological thinking teaches us there's a place in the mind where there is no karma, thus no fear; the Spiritual Mind.

The concept of stress is so ingrained in our lives, that *we have come to accept it as normal,* as a part of, "A Day In The Life." For example; we come home wiped out at the end of a bad work day, and we say, "you won't believe what a stressful day I had." *But, we don't say* "you won't believe what a fearful day I had." This is because we don't dare admit to ourselves, what we are experiencing is fear, that what we are really afraid of is: *our self perception of ourself,* of the ego karmic person we have become conditioned to think we are.

Stress occurs because we have been karma conditioned to believe we are karmic ego beings. So, the answer is not to deny our everyday stress, that's insanity, but rather to come to see that we are just experiencing, or watching, or observing, mental expressions of stress. The insightful Virginia Wolf quote on page 6 said it all: "You cannot find peace by avoiding life."

So what can we do to release stress, to re-find our peaceful mind? We can, with peaceful, determined, loving effort, realizing there will be ups and downs, begin again, and yet again, remembering: we are spiritual beings having a human experience.

We can do our best to regularly use Watcher/Chooser Mind, to remember the place in the mind, beyond the physical world: the Spiritual Mind. And, I want to say again, not deny the stress we feel in our everyday world, instead, we should accept we are trying to do something very difficult, yet the simplest of things, remember what we've never forgotten: True Identity.

Invite fear thoughts to come visit anytime; *they want to be loved.* So love them as you would a beautiful, small crying child. And then choose again, let Spiritual Mind embrace them. Stress, fear, anxiety, self-doubt, anger, conflict, are all the same; manifestations of ego-karma, some form of inner conflict, unwatched, unconscious, inner war. Stress is the energy eater, enemy of a good nights sleep. Stress's only value is to be seen, to be let go of, removed. Stress is fear. "Fear is the mind killer."

History has a short memory, it remembers everything as if it were happening now.

The ego mind is like a car that won't start, but keeps going backwards.

"I never got angry with my guitar, 'cause when I strike a chord it gives me what I wanna hear." *B.B. King, "I Like To Live The Love"*

Is the glass half empty or half full? It depends on who's looking at it.

"You may believe that you are responsible for what you do, but not for what you think. The truth is you are responsible for what you think, because it is only at this level that you can exercise *choice*. What you do comes from what you think." *A Course In Miracles.*

Every instant of ego life, we have a chance to choose: Spiritual Mind or Button Mind, war or peace.

"After waiting an eternity to be born, I came into the world, bound and entangled with knotted ropes." **Nino Provenzano**, *from his book "Footprints In The Snow"*

"Problems cannot be solved by the same thinking we used when we created them." *Albert Einstein*

We can't negotiate with karma, other choices are available, negotiation just isn't one of them.

To study neurology separate from psychology is like to trying to eat with your mouth closed.

"Dress Worn by Princess Diana Sells for a Record $1.15 Million" *NYT 12/19/23*

Ego consciousness created the concept of a "karmic unconscious mind," to give on-going birth to itself. In this way, it hides from its own unreality by creating conflict, using both dream and split physical sub-personalities. This self created process keeps it occupied resolving the karmic issues it has created.

If we don't learn to stand on our own two feet, others will stand on them for us.

Relying on your ego-karma-history-conditioned mind for decisions about what to do in your everyday life is like playing ping-pong with yourself, always playing on, never accepting defeat.

"I had learned in the meanwhile the greatest and most important problems of life are all in a certain sense insoluble. They can never be solved, but only outgrown." *Carl Jung*

Instant Karma isn't gonna get you, as John sang, it's already got you.

I used to worry a lot, now, I don't worry that much anymore. And you know what, I'm worried about that.

Whatever you're thinking about another person, you are *first* giving those thoughts to yourself - as well as creating more karma. You can't be angry at someone, or unforgiving of someone, without being angry, without being unforgiving of yourself. If you're angry and screaming at someone, you're screaming at you.

When my hair has turned to gray, when my need for sex has faded away, I'll know I couldn't have learned love's meaning without bodies getting in the way.

"It's been my impression we come into the world as children who want love. And, if we can't get love, we settle for power." *Jean Bolen, Jungian Analyst*

Ego mind always searches for clues as to the beginning of its existence to prove it exists.

The house was burning down, still some people inside ran around locking the doors.

Button karma mind is the past.

"There are people in the world so hungry, that God cannot appear to them except in the form of bread." *Mahatma Gandhi*

"My love belongs to those who can see it." *George Harrison*

Take time to Observe and Choose

"Don't you let nobody take you to a low level, just keep on, and keep on, until you reach higher ground."
Stevie Wonder, "Higher Ground"

You can't save someone who's drowning if they think they're swimming.

The difference between ego-karma mind and zoo animals is ego-karma mind will never acknowledge there are bars.

Ego-karma is a doom with a view.

Ego mind, our past accumulated karmic thoughts, reveal themselves to us in our dreams, as inner dream characters, as sub-personalities, needing to be seen, and then, without guilt, lovingly let go of, released. They reveal the split off parts of our ego-karmic personality *that motivate everyday behavior choices.* To deny or hide from them is to hide from ourselves.

"Sometimes religion gets in the way of God." *Bono*

Time is what keeps the light from reaching us. There is no greater obstacle to God than time. *Meister Eckhart*

We can't choose what we're watching, but we can choose how we want to watch.

In this one instant, as you are reading this, all events of history are combined as one.

Father Demo Square
Carmine and Bleecker, Greenwich Village

It seemed by karmic accident,
if you believe in accidents,
that those of us who were there,
happened to be there.

After it was over I thought . . .
had he ever been a working man,
did he have a wife, children, was he ever a free man?

"Over and out" those were the last words he said;
closed his eyes, slight tip of the head.

"Over and out," those were last words he said,
suddenly lying there dead,
dead on that cold-hard-wood karmic
Greenwich Village bench bed.

It was Sixth and Bleeker,
Father Demo Square, those of us there
said one last mass, raised one last glass for a
"Mr. Tambourine Man" one man band.

"How does it feel
To be on your own
With no direction home,
Like a complete unknown
Like a rolling stone?"

From "Like A Rolling Stone," Bob Dylan

39

"All the lonely people,
Where do they all come from?
All the lonely people,
Where do they all belong?"
From Eleanor Rigby, the Beatles

Think about Holden Caulfield, and then *consciously*
try to love everybody today, everybody you see today,
coming through the rye.

A book about the ego mind should be all blank pages."
Steve Cooper

Thinking we're ego-karmic human beings, living in
bodies, could be compared to getting dressed and
undressed at the same time.

Ego mind and karma are already finished, undone,
because they never begun.

Ego mind trusts only in its own emptiness. It thinks it
loves and trusts only in that, and in nothing else. In this
way, it comes to believe in itself, as the way, and the
truth, and the life.

The ego-karmic mind is a desert.
Flowers can't grow in a desert.
*"And my eyes fill with sand
As I scan this wasted land"*

From "Kashmir,: Led Zeppelin

40

The old know many things about love,
perhaps the young do not.

"For age is opportunity no less
than youth itself,
Though in another dress.
And as the evening twilight fades away,
The sky is filled with stars,
Stars invisible by day."
Henry Wadsworth Longfellow

"Good and bad, I define these terms
Quite clear, no doubt, somehow
Ah, but I was so much older then
I'm younger than that now."
From "My Back Pages," Bob Dylan

Karmic mind imagined an orphanage, named it "the world."

Whatever loving or otherwise thoughts, you think about others, you first give yourself.

Watcher/Chooser mind teaches us to: Express our love
to those we've *chosen* to come here to hear,
to those we've *chosen* to come here to see,
to give love to all, but devotion
only to those devoted to thee.

Ego mind only sees through the past. And in that seeing, creates its future . . . like a rolling stone.

Ego-karma mind is an echo chamber.

"The best political, social, and spiritual work we can do is to withdraw the projection of our shadow onto others." *Carl Jung*

"Learn to get in touch with the silence within yourself and know that everything in this life has a purpose. There are no mistakes, no coincidences. All events are blessings given to us to learn from." *Elizabeth Kübler-Ross*

The Many Faces Of Paradise

The many faces of paradise, I saw them all today!
I saw them on their bikes,
on the street, in the supermarket,
On the always crowded, overcrowded,
I - 4 Freeway.

They were disguised as ordinary folks,
Folks just like you and me, living their normal lives
On just another Costco, iPhone,
go to work, fill up the tank day.
The many, many, many faces of paradise.
I saw them all today!

"Anyone who has ever struggled with poverty knows how extremely expensive it is to be poor." *James Baldwin*

The ego/karma mind is like a car that won't start, but keeps going backwards.

"Inventions have eliminated so much of distance and time; for better, for worse, we are now each of us part of the surge and swell of great economic and political movements, and whatever we do, as individuals or as nations, deeply affects everyone else." *Vera Brittain, 1900-1925, "Testament Of Youth"*

A declaration of karma independence is needed.

Attention men and women: " *I am a spiritual being having an ego physical experience. I am not an OBJECT that needs to be empowered by my breast size!*" 😡

Susan K. also asked me to also include this quote: "I speak not only for women, but for men as well," she went on, "I mean their milk glands, why do we women think we have to show everyone what our milk glands look like? And how big they are, or aren't? Their only purpose is to feed babies! Maybe that's why men like to look at them, and why we like to show them, I don't know, I mean, what are we hungry for?"

-

Revealed bodies, one, two, three, every day we see.
Revealed hearts, ah, that's not done so easily.

"A culture fixated on female thinness is not an obsession about female beauty, but an obsession about female obedience. Dieting is the most potent political sedative in women's history; a quietly mad population is a tractable one." *Naomi Wolf, The Beauty Myth*

Ego invented fashion, to make itself look good to itself, to make itself look different, to make some parts of itself look the same, to make some parts of itself look different, but always to hide what was never there.

"She's the kind of a girl who makes the news of the world, yes you could say she was attractively built, yea, yea, yea." *From "Polyethylene Pam, the Beatles*

Overworking, A Psychological Ego Illness

Work and acquiescence to its "self created busyness," has become the primary way (there are many others such as drinking, over eating, smoking, sexual addiction, too much coffee, Facebook, anti-aging, 'what a day I've had,' etc.) in which we have found a method to avoid acknowledging the forgotten side of our personality. Work has become a way we rate and justify our very existence, meaning and purpose.

The ego-karma mind has made work and its various results such as: money saved, being liked, success attained, prestige, hours put in, designer clothing, being 'strong,' knowing the 'right' people, etc., a modern and shared false "God Judge," to be worshiped, to be looked to for redemption.

"If we could read the secret history of our enemies we should find in each man's life sorrow and suffering enough to disarm all hostility." *Henry Wadsworth Longfellow*

"I have no faith in human perfectibility. I think that human exertion will have no appreciable effect upon humanity. Man is now only more active - not more happy - nor more wise, than he was 6000 years ago." *Edgar Allan Poe*

Wanting to go faster in spiritual work is similar to saying, I could get to work a lot quicker if it weren't for these darn traffic lights.

Karma is a *wallpaper door, built by the ego mind.
The phrase "wallpaper door," is by Lewis Hyde. It is used in his introduction to Rainer Maria Rilke's book "Letters To A Young Poet."

Ego mind has a PhDenial.

Only those who feel they are losers have the insatiable need to win, to keep winning.

"Isn't it a pity? Now isn't it a shame, How we break each other's hearts, cause each other pain. How we take each other's love without thinking anymore. Forgetting to give back, isn't it a pity?" *George Harrison "Isn't It A Pity"*

Difficulty sleeping is incorrectly named, it should be called ego-somnia.

"If we wish to diminish the love of money which, we are told, is the root of all evil, the first step must be the creation of a system in which everyone has enough and no one has too much." *Bertrand Russell*

I had a dream. In it my friends said; "It's time to sleep to help you remember who you are. When you wake you'll think you're very small, it's part of the plan. This time you'll think you're a man." You'll be back before you know it.

Heaven is our inter-dependent Original Spiritual Mind, which is mutually shared, each different, yet the same.

The purpose of this book could be said to be: bringing the psychology and philosophy of Eastern spiritual thinking to the Western mind.

> I'm beside my self
> when I'm not beside you
> I don't know what to do
> when I am not beside you.
> I don't want to be beside myself
> I want to be beside you

Memory is a karma skill ego has taught us.

"Distance yourself from the people that you don't want to become. *Shane Parish*

"There is not a heart that exists in your human world that, if it were assured of safety, would not open instantly. It is all an issue of fear. You fear to love an imperfect world." *Emanuel's Book, Book One*

"Attitude is a choice. Happiness is a choice. Optimism is a choice. Kindness is a choice. Giving is a choice. Respect is a choice. Whatever choice you make makes you. Choose wisely." *Roy T. Bennett,*

Heaven is where we each have a Spiritual Birthright, each with a constant-mutual, yet distinctive Light.

This body is not me, I am not limited by this body, I am life without boundaries. I have never been born, and I have never died. *Thich Nhat Hanh*

"The timeless in you is aware of life's timelessness. And knows that yesterday is but today's memory and tomorrow is today's dream." *Khalil Gibran, The Prophet*

"Courage is the most important of all the virtues because without courage, you can't practice any other virtue consistently." *Maya Angelou*

"Unexpressed emotions will never die. They are buried alive, and will come forth later in uglier ways." *Sigmund Freud*

Ego mind thought it could create a material universe. Then it created humans, then it created karma, all to assure itself that it was all real.

Anne was 14

From: "The Diary of a Young Girl, Anne Frank"
This was written Saturday, July 15, 1944

"I have one outstanding character trait that must be obvious to anyone who's known me for any length of time: I have a great deal of self-knowledge. In everything I do, *I can watch myself as if I were a stranger.* I can stand across from the everyday Anne and, without being biased or making excuses, *watch* what she's doing, *both the good and the bad.* This self-awareness never leaves me, and every time I open my mouth, I think, you should have said that differently, or, that's fine the way it is.

I condemn myself in so many ways that I'm beginning to realize the truth of Father's adage: 'Every child has to raise itself.' Parents can only advise their children or point them in the right direction. Ultimately, people shape their own characters. In addition, I face life with an extraordinary amount of courage. I feel so strong and capable of bearing burdens, so young and free! When I first realized this, I was glad, because it means I can more easily withstand the blows life has in store."

It is believed that Anne died, February or March 1945, Bergen-Belsen concentration camp, Nazi Germany.

Anne was 15.

Karma is a cause and effect historical hallway of old,
It has no floor, no ceiling, no window,
no wall, no door.
Karma is the greatest story never told of yore.

Love without peace is impossible. Peace without love
is impossible.

Karma is eating donuts for what's in the middle

Karma is chess for one.

"There's always the next big thing." *Ruth Rudy*

Capitalism was necessary. So was kindergarten.

The experience of our generation: capitalism will not
die a natural death. *Walter Benjamin*

The faster the ego mind runs against the wind, the
harder the wind blows.

The Pope denounced the scale of emissions from high-
consumption cultures and argued that the world's poor
are paying the price. Francis, who took the name of the
patron saint of ecology, stands out among popes in his
push to make environmentalism a core part of the
faith. *Washington Post, October 4, 2023*

Mantra: Mantra, a devout silent word, or short phrase,
containing the Fateful thing you want to think of.

We become what we think about, *as* we are thinking about it.

"I have been deeply impressed with the fact that the new thing presented by fate, seldom or never corresponds to conscious expectation." *Carl Jung*

If you repeat your mantra regularly, all your problems will solve themselves. *Swami Satchidananda*

Original Existence is where there is no space between anything, or any one, yet none are encumbered.

Memory is a skill we have taught ourselves to remember.

Anger, stress, frustration, disappointment, are all positive signs ego/karma mind is working perfectly.

Ego-karma consciousness established the idea of a conflicted unconscious mind so it could hide from its own unreality. It hides by keeping busy creating, and then resolving, everyday life conflicted issues it has created. At the same time it creates new ones to be resolved.

If the Creator has no unconscious mind, can we?

"Bungalow Billy," now he wasn't silly, he wasn't just willy-nilly, he was a real karma killer-dilly! From the Beatles song, "Bungalow Bill'

A cause automatically becomes an effect waiting to happen. The question is not will it happen, but rather how and when will it happen. *"Every effect had a cause."* Dalai Lama, from the movie "Kundun"

"Living in the world can be a prison or a classroom."
Kenneth Wapnick, Ph.D.

Peace and love are inseparable twins.

Dear reader, just like you, I'm practicing too.

Aging - anti-aging - being young - growing old, it's all a ruse, a clever camouflage created by ego-karma mind to make our karmic dream seem like it has a short fuse.

Ego mind only sees through the past. And in that seeing, creates its future, *once-upon-time*, like a rolling stone.

Indian Summer is a moment in the mind that comes 'round every time you repeat mantra.

"I am he, as you are he, as you are me, and we are all together." *"I Am The Walrus,"* Beatles

One night, a perfectly white, bright, round, fog bound moon, rose up ever so slowly, behind a mountain sky. A little boy I used to know, in his bed, watching it all curiously from his bedroom window, spoke aloud to himself: "I wonder if teacher, or Mommy, or Daddy, I wonder if they know what that's all about?"

"The unconscious pursuit of ignorance creates
uncountable billions of worlds from one mind."
Wes Gibson

"The world of time is the world of illusion. What
happened long ago seems to be happening now."
A Course In Miracles

No matter who we talk to, we talk to ourselves first.

Ego-karma mind convinced us we have to make love.
We don't, we can't; we already have love, are love.

Due to cause-and-effect, karma is every thought you
will ever have, unless you find a way to realize you are
just watching, and then *consciously choose* differently.

Nothing you see, or experience, or feel, has any
meaning other than what you give it.

Vengeance is conflict. Karma is conflict. Karma is ego.

If you didn't have a mind, you wouldn't have any
DNA, or any genetic traits, or even a body. Everything
starts in the mind.

The brain does not feel, or love, or even think. It
responds only to whatever operating thought system
we choose to put in it, and then update it with. It's like
a MacBook, whatever operating system we enter, we
get back.

"The unconscious mind is the unwritten history of mankind from time unrecorded." *Carl Jung*

"It isn't until you come to a spiritual understanding of who you are – not necessarily a religious feeling, but deep down, the spirit within – that you can begin to take control." *Oprah Winfrey*

When someone pushes your button, you've found your karma.

You can't lose your mind, you can however misplace it.

"Mindfulness is the art of experiencing nonexistence of the past and the future." *Mokokoma Mokhonoana*

Understanding the meaning of love is the progressive realization of inter-dependent Origination.

Organic is not only a table set, it's a mind set.

"Even if we were in Heaven, we wouldn't be able to see it, if there is hell in our mind." *Carl Jung*

Danger

To deny danger is foolish. To see danger for what it is, is a way to be free. In all things there is a time to wait, there is a time to be cautious, there is a time to be bold.

It's a lucky thing smoking doesn't cause cancer, or by now millions of people would have stopped producing cigarettes for millions of other people to smoke.

Ego mind is a narcissist that doesn't love itself. Acting accordingly, it despises itself for it.

"The only advice that one person can give another about reading is to take no advice, to follow your instincts, to use your own reason, to come to your own conclusions." *Virginia Woolf*

The right method for the wrong person, is the wrong method.

When we find the certainty in uncertainty, we will certainly have found certainty.

History is ego mispelled.

"All the greatest and most important problems of life are fundamentally not solvable. They can never be solved, but only outgrown." *Carl Jung*

The best of things can't be planned.

Peace is the only thing worth fighting for, and you can't fight for peace.

God's will is simply for peace of mind. For only with peace of mind, can we know God's will.

Love of money is an old story, always between strangers.

Narcissism is a fancy word for fear. It say's: I can't trust anyone to love me, so I'll just love myself, because no one can do it better.

I've become more patient lately, I've found things happen faster that way.

Ego-karma mind is a mask hiding a recurring series of spiritual pandemics.

Hope and faith went for a swim. Faith learned to swim before diving in.

We shouldn't worry about what may happen in the future, but we should prepare. How to prepare and what to prepare for is the question.

Those we meet in our dreams, who are they? What is the meaning of what they say?

Fear is a reflection of the unconscious mind watching itself.

Music speaks with certainty about what words only hint.

Karma is ego thought plaque. Brush! Floss!

Colors, your colors: all of them,
Yellow, black, blue, and green,
Tell me of them, all you've been,
all you've seen;
Since you were 17.

Don't leave anything out, leave everything in.
Fill me up, fill me in. Tell me of your ballet.
Tell me when your young hair began to gray.

Tell me of your dreams, your schemes,
your regrets; your should haves, could haves,
Your . . . if I only knew then's.

I want to know it all,
all you've done; all you've seen,
Since we were 17.

Mantra Womantra

Gonna' say it in   sunlight,
gonna' say it in   moonlight,
Gonna' say it, and say it
anytime I feel it's right.

Gonna' say it in the morning,
gonna' say it in the night,
Gonna' say it and say it,
until I get it right.

Gonna' say it again,
just like I said it before,
Gonna' say it until there's
no need to say it any more.

Gonna' say it, and say it,
until I finally forget
what sayin' it was for.

Take time to observe, you are the Watcher.

We can tell how disorganized we are, by how long it takes us to get organized.

It is a necessary journey karmic humans have set upon.
And who shall inspire us?
Women, women in modest dress,
for many have come empty of love, sounding the call.

The ego mind created the physical world and then karma. How was ego mind created?

"The outstanding faults of the economic society we live are: its failure to provide for full employment, and its arbitrary and inequitable distribution of wealth and incomes." *John Maynard Keynes. Mr. Keynes, a British economist whose ideas fundamentally affected the theory and practice of modern macroeconomics, is considered the 20th century's most influential economist.1883-1946.*

There are no buttons in the present moment, except those we *choose* to bring with us.

Karma is the whitest shade of pale.

Some people can predict the future because it's already happened.

After all is said and done cause-and-effect are one.

Everything seems to go slower when we're in a hurry.

The only thing to be convinced of regarding your ego-karmic unconscious mind is: it's unconscious - and is directing your behavior.

"They gathered for the feast, they stab it with their steely knives, but they just can't kill the beast." *The Eagles, "Hotel California" Dear reader, what do you suppose the Eagles were referring to?*

The ego is self inflicted psychological cold war.

Ego mind is a lawyers dodge.

"Among all my patients in the second half of life that is to say over 35, there has not been one who's problem in the last resort was not that of finding a religious outlook on life. This of course has nothing whatever to do with the particular creed or membership of the church." *Carl Jung*

For different reasons, neither peace nor ego negotiate.

"What if God was one of us? Just a slob like one of us? Just a stranger on the bus trying to make his way home?" *Joan Osborne, "One Of Us"*

The ego mind keeps running in place wondering when it will arrive at its destination.

"We are what we feel and perceive. If we are angry, we are the anger." *Thich Nhat Hanh*

"May the long time sun shine upon you, all love surround you, and the pure light within you guide you on your way." *Used as a Yogic chant*

To get out of ego mind, we first have to become well informed as to how we got in.

We are more afraid of solitude than anything else, afraid of what we might become aware of, what we might hear about, lurking unseen in ourselves.

"We love to learn we're not alone." Inspired by the movie *"Shadowlands"*

"We cannot swim for new horizons until you have courage to lose sight of the shore." *William Faulkner*

"Anger is an acid that can do more harm to the vessel in which it is stored than to anything on which it is poured." *Mark Twain - quoted from Psychology Today*

Should any two decide and truly desire with all their heart, to consciously practice non-judgmentally loving each other, no matter the perceived cost, a relationship path to peace has begun.

No matter who we talk to we always talk first to ourselves.

"We shall not cease from journeying
And the end of all our journeying
Will be to arrive where we started
Knowing the place for the first time."
T.S. Eliot

Ego mind is a psychological coma.

As we learn to see others egos as our own, we help
so called others in that way.

"It's better to lose your ego to the one you love, than to
lose the one you love to your ego." *John Keats*

When the student is ready the ego appears.

Humanity toils onward,
enamored of its own helplessness,
fixing problems that can't be fixed,
seeking answers to questions that don't exist.

Time will never end; what never began cannot end.

We are fragments of ego-karmic long ago's,
forgotten centuries of Sunday's,
frightened fragments of below and above,
we are hollow, fictitious,
we seek unknowingly for versions of broken love.

"I was educated once — it took me years to get over
it." *Mark Twain*

"Forgive yourself for not knowing
what you didn't know
before you learned it."
Maya Angelou

"Your Remedy is within you, but you do not sense it.
Your Sickness is from you, but you do not perceive it.
Therefore, you have no need to look beyond yourself,
What you seek is within you, if only you reflect."
Ali ibn Abi Talib

"You have to grow from the inside out. None can teach
you; none can make you spiritual. There is no other
teacher but your own soul." *Swami Vivekananda*

"You have your way. I have my way. As for the right
way, the correct way, and the only way, it does not
exist." *Friedrich Nietzsche*

It's possible to be someone we don't want to be, to live
a life we don't want to live, and to live it for so long,
that we forget we're living it, and to think we like it.

We can run from ourselves, we can run from others,
we can even run from God. But run we cannot from
the consequences of our choices.

You can't tame the tiger, but you can leave the jungle.

There's only one thing to remember. There's only one
thing to forget.

Karma mind made-up an orphanage; named it "world."

War and peace are opposites. Spiritual Mind has no
opposite.

Marriage is an ego-karmic idea. What was never separated cannot be joined.

Difficulty sleeping should be called: ego-somnia.

"Peace does not mean to be in a place where there is no noise, trouble or hard work. It means to be in the midst of those things and still be calm in your heart."
A quote on a cup I bought.

Fear is the one emotion of the separated ego, and it's created karma. It lives in fear of being found out.

Ego mind loves only itself. Ego mind knows not of love.

If too many people become upscale, ego mind will invent upper-upscale!

I found a missing umbrella in my pillowcase. It's hard to sleep in the rain, but sometimes I had to because the weather was so bad. Weather is unpredictable.

Only in growing old we fully experience what it feels like being young, as well as benefits accrued to both.

Time passes slowly when one is in a hurry.

Heaven is a place where everyone is the same but with a different Light.

What is the sound of one hand clapping? We'll know when we hear it.

I thought of this one day walking down Bleecker in the Village. The street we live on, it's like all streets, it's neutral. It doesn't care what stores or houses we build on it. Or if we don't build anything on it. It doesn't care if we walk on it or not, if we change its name, if we change its size and shape. But no matter what we do, a street will always be a street. Ego mind is a street like that, a street with no address.

Fear is the unconscious mind, and it is capable only of remembering itself, yet is afraid of remembering itself.

Is there a deep state? Yes, a deep state that threatens all humanity, because individually and collectively it's shared. It is purely psychological, Western psychology calls it the unconscious, Yogic psychology calls it the ego-karmic bag.

"Prayer is not asking. It is a longing of the soul. It is daily admission of one's weakness. It is better in prayer to have a heart without words than words without a heart." *Mahatma Gandhi*

"So fine was the morning except for a streak of wind here and there that the sea and sky looked all one fabric, as if sails were stuck high up in the sky, or the clouds had dropped down into the sea." *Virginia Woolf*

"What I am looking for is not out there, it is in me."
Helen Keller

There's one thing we know for sure about the unconscious; it's unconscious. Which means we don't know anything about it.

"Die the death of the ego and be reborn spiritually even in this very life." *Swami Prahavananda*

If you want to really get to know the ego face-to-face, belly to belly, try going on a diet.

Chess is an ego mind game where one tries to think of every possible move which has already happened, both before and after it happened. AI is HYPER-IZED chess.

Karma is a circle. So no matter where you go, you will meet yourself coming back.

Karma is where the ego came to believe it can live and die.

In spiritual practice if we try too hard, ego mind is involved. And, if we don't try hard enough, ego mind is involved.

Karma it's like a twisted pretzel that gets bigger every time you take a bite.

Checkers for one, don't mind if I do.
Checkers for one, I know all the right moves.
Checkers for one,
even when I win, I lose.

Ego mind doesn't want to forget it has nothing to remember.

Everyone who has an ego should receive an Academy Award for acting like someone they're not.

Good news to the kamic-ego mind is something like going to the oral surgeon and being told you don't need a root canal; but you need your gums removed.

Observe and choose anew, oftentimes.

Without faith and love, prayer is a chair without legs.

One religion, like a single type of food, cannot satisfy everybody." *Dalai Lama from his book "In My Own Words"*

Everything depends on inner change; when this has taken place, then, and only then does the world change. *Martin Buber*

Each one of us has our own evolution of life, and each one of us goes through different tests which are unique and challenging. But certain things are common. And we do learn things from each other's experience. On a spiritual journey, we all have the same destination. *A. R. Rahman*

The Piano Tuner

The ego mind resembles an antique piano keyboard
with numberless-numbers of keys, all out of tune.

The keyboard itself doesn't believe it's out of tune. It
refuses to accept that each key must learn to play, in its
own way, yet in tune with all the others.

The keyboard refuses to be tuned! It wants to play
whatever it wants, whenever it wants, however it
wants. It doesn't care about any of the other keys.

The piano tuner, is the only one who knows the
harmonization method; is aware of this piano, as well
as an amaranthine number of other pianos, with more
or less the same tuning issue, but still never tells them
when, or how, or what to play.

Instead the tuner employs volunteer tuners who've
mastered various tuning methods, for various
keyboards, making them available, but only when
asked, to provide lessons.

Tuners tune, players play.
Old players, old keyboards,
we all just play and play, play and play;
until there's nothing left to play.

A barely ten year old Hopi girl said, "When it is quiet, really quiet here, we'll all be with God, the Navahos and us, and the Anglos. The land will be with God, and not with us." "Our people are here to wait until the time comes that no one hurts the land; then we will be told we've done our job and we can leave." *This was a barely ten year old Hopi girl talking to Dr. Robert Coles, from his book, "The Spiritual Life Of Children."* 🖤

"When flowers bloom bees come uninvited."
Ramakrishna

In the ego-karma world, there's only one meaningful relationship to remember, and that is because all one's other relationships derive from this one.

To a garbage bag, garbage is garbage. Ego mind is a psychological garbage bag.

Seeing with ego-karma is like wearing glasses with the wrong prescription.

Ego mind is what you feel like when you get a parking ticket and don't own a car.

The material world was not made to work.

"Can't say what I'm doing here
But I hope to see much clearer,
after living in the material world"
"Living In The Material World," George Harrison,

Ego minds ability to care for us is comparable to getting a root canal from a foot doctor.

"Ego mind is invisible to those who can't see it."
Meryl S., New York

"Peace is present here and now, in our selves, and in everything we do and see. The question is whether or not we are in touch with it." *Thich Nhat Hanh*

Ego mind created genetics as a distraction.

Ego-karma mind is that sinking feeling in your stomach when you miss the exit on the Interstate, in heavy traffic, you're late for an appointment, and the next exit is 12 miles away.

If the Tao can help you on your chosen pathway, *"The Secret Of The Golden Flower"* should be part of your spiritual dossier; the one with Richard at the Wilhelm.

Ego mind is a like getting a great deal on a car that doesn't have a steering wheel.

Ego mind is its own best friend. Ego mind has no friends.

If you feel you're not doing your best, ask your Inner Teacher to help you. In that way you can be assured, you have done your best, and have been helped. Being helped is a process. To ask is to be helped.

Doing what we see as best is measurable. Asking for help from the Inner Teacher is beyond measurement.

Only In The Movies

Only in the movies
Can someone get shot in the head,
Stabbed in the back, kicked in the face,
And then come back and play another scene.

What are we watching?
Why do so many of us like watch?
When does fiction become kerosene?

When karma is involved, our every day functions of love, reason, and compromise, become karmatose.

At what age should we 55/65+ year olds no longer hesitate to show our gray? Whose approval, whose love, whose "I'm OK" are we looking for anyway? Since time waits for no one, we'd best get on with it.

We become what we fight with.

"One man practicing kindness in the wilderness is worth all the temples this world pulls." *Jack Kerouac, The Dharma Bums*

I'm working on giving up taking the long way home, across the park, through the wind and the rain, it's not so much the distance, as it is the pain.

The ego causes its own insurrection.

Karma is the world clock, always running backwards.

Capitalism does not care for capitalists, only for itself.

The ego invented the symbol "King" so it could worship at its own throne.

The official next half of ego/karma life begins when puberty-personality encounters every day reality. If not resolved, adolescent personalities become old age fatalities.

Meditation is hatha yoga for the mind.

The ego is a comedian without a sense of humor that only laughs at its own jokes.

Ego always arrives on time for an appointment never made.

Stop often and watch your mind as it thinks. Keep in mind it's impossible to be what you're watching. So who is it that is watching? And what is being watched?

Deepak Chopra

"Anger is remembered pain, fear is anticipated pain, guilt is self directed pain, depression is depletion of energy. A cure-return is to love & joy."

"Every cell in your body is eavesdropping on your thoughts".

"A quiet mind is more important than a positive mind."

"Our minds influence the key activity of the brain, which then influences everything; perception, cognition, thoughts and feelings, personal relationships; they're *all* a projection of you."

"We are not victims of aging, sickness and death. These are part of scenery, not the seer, who is immune to any form of change. This seer is the spirit, the expression of eternal being."

"Life gives you plenty of time to do whatever you want to do if you stay in the present moment."

"Before a brain can register a thought, a mind must think it... every step of the way is mind over matter... We override our brains all the time."

"The world sometimes feels like an insane asylum. You can decide whether you want to be an inmate or pick up your visitor's badge."

Simone de Beauvoir (1908–1986)

"There is only one solution if old age is not to be an absurd parody of our former life, and that is to go on pursuing ends that give our existence meaning."

"Harmony between two individuals is never granted, it has to be conquered indefinitely."

Change your life today. Don't gamble on the future, act now, without delay.

"Whatever the country, capitalist or socialist, man was everywhere crushed by technology, made a stranger to his own work, imprisoned, forced into stupidity. The evil all arose from the fact that he had increased his needs rather than limited them; . . . As long as fresh needs continued to be created, so new frustrations would come into being.

When had the decline begun? The day knowledge was preferred to wisdom and mere usefulness to beauty. . . . Only a moral revolution - not a social or political revolution - only a moral revolution would lead man back to his lost truth."

"If we had no faults of our own, we should not take so much pleasure in noticing those in others."

"If we have not peace within ourselves, it is in vain to seek it from outward sources."

Swami Prabhavananda

"My master used to tell us: the breeze of God's grace is always blowing, set your sail to catch this breeze."

"There are many theories as to the origin of religion. The Vedantic theory is that it springs from man's desire to transcend the limitations and bondages of life."

"We are longing for the infinite, and our thirst can never be quenched in the finite. This great lesson, we all must learn, sooner or later: the one motive behind all our struggles and striving is the desire to reach the infinite."

"In the language of the Upanishads, Brahman, or God, is Sat-chit-ananda. Sat is eternal being, immortal life. Chit is pure consciousness, infinite wisdom. Ananda is love and abiding happiness."

-

Ego's only goal is to deny the awful emptiness of its perceived loss of Spiritual Mind.

Ego plans ahead by looking back.

Ego is an escape hatch leading back in.

Being physically naked and psychologically naked with another are as different as hot water and ice.

The ego is a no-show that showed up.

"Every effect had a cause."
"Non-violence takes a long time."
Dalai Lama from the movie "Kundun"

Inside every angry ego adult lives a frightened child, afraid of love, afraid to love, afraid it may not be there.

Without faith and love prayer is like a chair without legs.

Ego mind is authoritarianism that always thinks it is right.

Four handed piano is a good way to play the spiritual relationship song. Each player plays part of the same song, each in their own way.

There is a perfect way to stay calm as a monk, become a calm monk.

We can't see what isn't there, but we try, until trying becomes to difficult, becomes to brutal to try. *Only then,* we try to find another way to see what isn't there.

Swami Satchidananda gave a word of advice, Mantra.

Mantra is just one of many methods of using a short verse, affirmation and/or prayer, of asking to be led out of the desert.

"You must have a spirit of prayer, or you will find it hard to persevere. Pray with great faith in God, and God will take care of everything." *Mother Theresa*

Inner Or Outer Fatalities

"No one develops their personality because somebody tells them it would be useful or advisable to do so. The developing personality obeys no caprice, no command, no insight, only brute necessity. It needs the motivating force of inner or outer fatalities." *Carl Jung*

-

If there's no end in sight, we're looking in the wrong direction.

Knowing that by the process of 'thought accumulation' we become what we think about, let us each without judgment, self condemnation regret, or fear of punishment, ask ourselves: What are we thinking about now, at this moment?

Karma will end when mine is yours,
when yours is mine.
When there are no more
peace treaties left to sign.
When there are no more words left to rhyme.
When mine is yours, when yours is mine.

The ego, believing it had, and thus was capable of, separating from its Creator, created perpetual personal karma to assure it self of its own continued existence.

"Enlightenment is ego's ultimate disappointment."
Chögyam Trungpa

Harry, a priest, said to C.S. Lewis regarding his wife's illness: "I know how hard you've been praying and now God is answering. Lewis responded: That's not why I pray Harry. I pray because I can't help myself, I pray because I'm helpless, I pray because the need flows out of me all the time, waking and sleeping. It doesn't change God it changes me."
From the movie "Shadowlands"

"Few things are more rewarding than a child's open uncalculating devotion." *Vera Brittain*

Ego is a word in a dictionary that doesn't exist.

Word is a symbol for something that doesn't exist.

"All negativity is caused by an accumulation of psychological time, and denial of the present."
Eckhart Tolle, The Power Of Now

The ego mind is like a bottomless empty plate of lasagna layers that always wants desert no matter how full it is. *Ann Marie L. Bonasera*

Ego not only knows the ropes, ego is the ropes.

Ego invented birth and death to brainwash itself that it exists.

Someone I hadn't seen for about 20 years said to me; "I don't care what you say about this guy named Harry Krishna, he's up to no good."

When the world has taught us enough, we will want to let go of all that the world has taught us.

If I only knew then what I know now, said the karmic butcher to the cow. The cow at a loss for words said: "Moooo."

"Mankind's greatest gift, also its greatest curse, is that we have free choice. We can make our choices built from love or from fear." *Elisabeth Kübler-Ross*

Democracy is a day to day progress report to humanity. It informs us as to how much we have evolved (or not) psychologically, spiritually, to a point where we can: *Consciously recognize that, we can choose to create an inter-dependent world to live in;* a world of peace and love between nations, a world of mutual prosperity for all, a world of inter-dependent origination - or not. Beginning first with ourselves.

The ego-karmic mind system is a circus that came to town and never left.

There are two days in the year that we cannot do anything, yesterday and tomorrow. *Mahatma Gandhi*

Karma plays no favorites.

Everything depends on inner change; when this has taken place, then, and only then does the world change. *Martin Buber*

Attention, ‼
Beethoven, Bach, Brahms, and Vivaldi, fans,
here they are again, oh, so cleverly disguised,
brought back by reincarnation's hippie demand:
Sergeant Karma's Lonely Hearts, Club Band!

With every thought we have a chance to choose to free
ourselves from our self created karma.

Karma is unceasing thought recycling, it goes on all
the time, day and night.

The way out of karma is to remember: choose again:
erase: repeat.

The only proof needed to show you that karma is real,
is that you think you are reading this.

Karma has a mind of its own, it's called the
unconscious.

Karma and justice will never rhyme.

There's a thought we can't figure out; peace of mind,
that's because as soon as we try it's gone.

"The only journey is the one within." *Rainer Maria Rilke*

Karma is in the eyes of the beholder.

I'm writing this for whoever happens to read it.

Karma has many thought manifestations, but only one source.

Think of what our life would be like if we had been walking backwards all the time, but thought we were walking forwards. That's what ego mind has us doing.

Everyday, someone, somewhere, gets up and says: I'm gonna' eat part of a chicken, a "Chicken, (with an) Egg and Cheese Muffin," over at "Chick-fil-A," then gonna' get some hot coffee, be on my way.
Approximately 9 billion chickens are killed every year. ASPCA

Find those karmic Holden's in you ready to fall off the cliff, find a way to catch them before they go over.

Choose anew.

Living unaware of karma is like wearing shoes one size too small for so long, and getting used to it, finally accepting it as normal.

Ego-karma is a 12-Step program to guarantee the continuation of past ego addictions.

Karma is inherently narcissistic, because all it can remember is itself.

If we've learned to do everything by the book, we should be sure we've read the right book.

Take time to Observe and Choose.

What is AI?

AI Is Ego-Karma.   AI is HAL 9000.

The most important consequential fact to understand
about AI, about artificial intelligence, is: It's artificial.
It isn't real. And it creates like itself.

AI is an exact duplication of its creator; ego-karma
mind. In Eastern psychology this mind is called the
"karmic mind." *It is the combined, interconnected, and
thus interactive total, of all thoughts in the ego-karma
mind since time, and thus history, began.* In Western
psychology it's called the unconscious mind. If you
want to get some idea of how it functions, and what
you know about it, try understanding your dreams.

Regarding ego-karma mind, time and thus history, if
you haven't yet, see pages 12-15, read what Einsteins
"Theory Of Relativity," the Dalai Lama, and David
Bohm, an American-born, British quantum physicist,
expert in neuropsychology theoretical physics, and
philosophy, have to say about time. They each join, in
both spiritual and scientific agreement, that time,
therefore history, therefore ego-karma mind, therefore
AI, were each born simultaneously in a "dream like,
unreal instant of time past" a moment that never
happened. In that instant, what is generally known as
the "Big Bang," the physical world seemed to be born.

Western psychology and philosophy say that the "Big Bang," was the beginning of time. So, we can say the "Big Bang" was the beginning of ego mind, of karma, of time, and their inseparable partner in history: cause and effect. And so like time, ego-karma mind seems to continue on, and on, but in fact does not exist, because it is not real, it is artificial.

AI Is: The computerized "digital compiling" of multiple sources of karmic thought information. This gathered information is then inputted into "computer minds," such as the *Google search engine. AI then makes what has been inputted, accessible to anyone who asks a question about anything in *that* search engine. Each search engine gives answers, *based only* on information inputted. So different search engines, with "certainty," will provide different answers, to the same questions, like humans do, change its opinions about things, like human ego mind does, and make *mistakes, just like the human ego mind does..
See page 85

AI is an extension of ego-karma-mind. Due to the boomerang "cause and effect" of karma, of one thought always causing another; *everything that's ever happened in the ego-karma mind, and its big bang creation, the physical world, has already happened.* So, AI is simultaneously both solving and creating all the problems the world is having both now, and in the future, and must, *to prove it's real, not artificial.*

Like a dog trying to catch its own tail, we are ghost authors of our own behavior, who keep going round and round on our karmic merry-go-round, as explained by Jung and Freud quotes, pages 14/15 of this book.

Now, we, the "technologically advanced" humans of our historical moment, are going to use AI, a duplicate version of the same ego-karmic mind intelligence system which created all our problems, to solve our problems, to make the world a better place. Since our false belief system, the *ego-k*arma mind, is the only problem, there is only one solution: Try to find a non-ego-karma mind thought system, to help re-mind us: We are spiritual beings having an AI experience.

"We cannot solve our problems with the same thinking we used when we created them." *Albert Einstein*

AI can be used to great advantage in areas such as the medical profession. But if the root cause of problems caused by ego-karma mind is not seen for what it is, and a solution found to undo it from its roots, the worlds current problem issues such as: War and peace relationship issues between nations, personal and business relationship issues, financial issues, racial issues, political issues which divide us, all ego mind psychological illnesses, all forms of physical illness, all problems of world hunger and poverty, suffering, *will repeatedly re-appear as if new,* waiting to be solved anew. Even if a dog could catch its own tail - what would the dog do with it when caught?

"Last week, *Google unveiled its biggest change to search in years, showcasing new artificial intelligence capabilities that answer people's questions in the company's attempt to catch up to rivals Microsoft and OpenAI. The new technology has since generated a litany of untruths and errors - including recommending glue as part of a pizza recipe and the ingesting of rocks for nutrients - giving a black eye to Google and causing a furor online." *New York Times, May 24, 2014*

Revenge is self perpetuating cause and effect.

"Your willingness to look at your darkness is what empowers you to change." *Iyanla Vanzant*

We should attempt being mindful of not taking others for granted, of calling others by their name, of always saying thank you, of treating others as we would like to be treated: but never more, never less, never instead. And remembering, there are no others.

As a result of cause and effect, karma goes backwards and forwards at the same time. This means, everything that has ever happened has already happened.

Until we learn to be alone with ourselves we shall always be alone.

"You are present at the birth of every thought you have." *Bob Dylan*

Has there ever been a system of government that has not produced conflict? The problem is not government, or legislations voted verdict. The problem is the cause of conflict: the unwatched mind.

We can't control ego-karma mind by trying to control ego-karma mind. As a result of cause and effect, karma goes backwards and forwards at the same time. This means, everything that has ever happened has already happened, and is happening again all the time.

"Therefore, send not to know
For whom the bell tolls,
It tolls for thee."
John Donne

We have chosen to be convinced we are soldiers of ego, of karma, of time and war.

Our belief in histories existence has habituated us into thinking we are ego's, that war and time are normal, and inevitable, and that the only way for us to protect ourselves from the enemy's outside ourselves, who are bent on our destruction, is to fight them. We have done this unconsciously since time never began, in this way, entrenching ego mind, denying Spiritual Mind.

Again and again; backwards to nowhere have we marched, certain of our progress, certain of our purpose, imprinting conflicted ego mind footprints deeper and deeper into the unconscious desert-karma sands of our shared collective and personal histories. Our belief in history, karma, that is to say the past, has so conditioned us to the inevitability of conflict, or war, that we have actually come to accept it as normal!

Ego mind, cleverly, deviously, has us signing peace treaties, while at the same time, it gives the green light to the normality of war by creating the rules or "The Laws of War," that as Wikipedia says: "Regulates the conditions for initiating war, and the conduct of warring parties."

In other words, ego mind is saying, that *in some circumstances war and killing* is justified, *but it must be regulated.* Ego mind also categorizes <u>some</u> acts of war, that is killing of others, as "war crimes."

In this way ego - via cause and effect - both justifies and perpetuates the continuing inevitability of war; saying war has always happened before, and will always happen, it's just a normal part of everyday life, like say, shopping, working, or having a car.

Because of the unwillingness of each of us as individuals, and thus humanity as a whole, to find a way to face and then choose to release our past karma buttons, we remain habituated "ego mind button addicts," addicted to the continuing need for conflict within ourselves, and then, rather than taking responsibility for our buttons, we see others outside ourselves as pushing them, and then we take revenge.

Without a *chosen* awareness of Spiritual Mind, we will continue our unaware, unconscious ego-karma tolling.

"Therefore, send not to know
For whom the bell tolls,
It tolls for thee."
John Donne

The problem of karma is people and places all will change, while all karma memories will stay the same.

Spiritual remembrance practice is everything. No effort is ever forgotten, wasted, unheard.

"The living moment is everything." *D.H. Lawrence*

Karma is craving for desert without a meal.

Mantra is a feather duster for karmic mind.

Who are those we meet in our dreams? Why do we meet them when we do? What are they doing? Why are they doing what they are doing? How should we interpret what they are doing? How did they get into our mind? Are we glad to meet them? Where do they come from? Why do some of us dream, and some do not? Is ego-karma involved? What of Spiritual Mind?

-

We earthlings live in an ego mind **Spiritual Utility Vehicle** we've named a body. With dedicated devotion we can learn to set our chosen **Guidance Peace System** to Spiritual Mind. So when the ego-karma mind **Spiritual Utility Vehicle** leads us astray, the **Global Peace System** will get back on our chosen way.

Living in karmic time is like being in a baseball game that's always tied, always in extra innings.

Where are we?
How many times have we tried?
How many gordian knots have we tied?

Why are we?
How many times have we slept?
How many tears have we wept?

Who are we?
How many homes have we had?
How many roads have we walked?

Where are we?
How many languages have we talked?
How many times have we died?

Why are we?

How many wars won? How many wars lost?
How many burdens found us helpless, hopeless,
star-crossed? How many times have we paid the cost?

Who are we?

Where are the enemies now, to whom we used to bow?
How much longer shall we attempt bargains with the
wind? How many more times will we sail off the end
of the earth seeking discovery of the new world?

Where are we? Why are we? Who are we?

Karma is everything you remember that never happened.

I didn't make my bed this morning and didn't feel guilty. I must be making spiritual progress!

"There is no such thing as a superiority complex, only an inferiority complex in disguise." *Sigmund Freud*

The ego mind is an impermanent form of spiritual dementia.

War is an ego mind sub-personality.

"It's been my impression we come into the world as children who want love. And if we can't get love, we settle for power." *Jean Bolen, Jungian Analyst*

This book is about finding out how to find peace of mind, after first discovering that you've never lost it.

The ego mind you call you, doesn't care about you.

What is karma? Karma is forgetting you're a spiritual being having a human experience.

Choose frequently, it will become a habit, and then work on its own, like any habit.

Whatever you repress you become. Whatever you accept and choose to let go of, you also become.

A Dream

A soft tan wallpaper covered wall,
a deep blue vase sitting on a dark-wood oak table,
amongst colors squared.

There in that safehold
all worlds colors were enclosed:
enclosed there in a single red rose.

Karma is overlooking the fact that you are a non-physical being having a physical experience.

"The spiritual journey is one of continuous learning and purification. When you know this, you become humble." *Sogyal Rinpoche*

"Just by the very nature of our birth, we are on the spiritual journey." Thomas Keating

Karma is what never happened happening again.

We're karma-tose until we're not.

Karma is artificial intelligence creating the physical world in its own image.

"How could there be a sin that exceeds God's love?"
Fyodor Dostoevsky, The Brothers Karamazov

"The individual has always had to struggle to keep from being overwhelmed by the tribe. If you try it, you will be lonely often, and sometimes frightened. But no price is too high to pay for the privilege of owning yourself." *Rudyard Kipling*

"The more one judges, the less one loves." *Honore de Balzac*

"The great acts of love are done by those who are habitually performing small acts of kindness."*Victor Hugo*

"What is hell? I maintain that it is the suffering of being unable to love." *Fyodor Dostoevsky*

Stress, disappointment, fear, guilt, sin, lack of love, deviously all appear different, yet are one and the same.

God, whatever we perceive God to be, does not have an unconscious or ego/karma mind, therefore neither can we. But we have convinced ourselves we do.

I knew my karmic life was at a tipping point when my GPS told me to check back later because all the team members were busy helping other drivers.

The ego/karma mind is a tattoo on a body that doesn't exist.

Karma is a spiritual mind hacker.

"He filled a shelf with a small army of books and read and read; but none of it made sense. They were all subject to various cramping limitations: those of the past were outdated, and those of the present were obsessed with the past." *Alexander Pushkin*

The ego is a false alarm that is always ringing.

Karma, the unconscious, created a cause and effect unreal physical world of personal and interpersonal conflict, to avoid seeing itself as the cause and effect of all conflict, thus avoiding seeing itself as both victim and victimizer.

Ego desert mind is an undercover form of self hate.

The spiritual journey is individual, highly personal. It can't be organized or regulated. It isn't true that everyone should follow one path. Listen to your own truth. *Ram Dass*

It's possible for us to be psychologically lost for so long that we forget we're lost, and experience being lost as normal.

"If you are willing to look at another person's behavior towards you as a reflection of the state of their relationship with themselves rather than a statement about your value as a person, then you will, over a period of time, cease to react at all." *Yogi Bhajan*

"A lot of parents will do anything for their kids except let them be themselves." *Banksy*

-

"The danger of motherhood, you relive your early self, through the eyes of your mother." *Joyce Carol Oates*

Work at become conscious of projecting another's karma, mistaking it for yours.

Desert ego mind personalities come in three forms; melting, freezing, frozen.

All stress is a form of repressed karma.

Karma is the illusion of winning.

Get up, try again, I have said to myself many times, get up start again, my tired of trying friend,

All physical thoughts originate in ego mind, including genetics. Without ego there are no genetics. If humanity wants to affect genetics, first it must affect ego mind.

Laws established by karmic humanity, have loopholes, ambiguities, that can be used by the scrupulous to circumvent the laws that ambiguity itself has created. A loophole is a convenient escape invented by lawyers for use when no escape is possible. As for ambiguities definition, it's hard to pin down.

You can't keep secrets from the unconscious mind.

There's only one reason we can have a splitting headache, we have a split mind.

If you feel like your boomerang won't come back, you've found your ego

Karma is a place you've never been to, getting there and saying: it's good to be back again.

Old karmic habits are hard to break, especially the ones we don't know we have.

Anything you find helpful in this book use, anything you don't, into the garbage. Piece of cake.

Denying what's seen physically is lunacy. Thinking it's real, spiritual atrophy.

You can't organize religion.

Have you noticed the Holden Caulfield in your desert ego mind, peeping through the blinds?

Here have we come once more, looking for the keys to an unlocked door.

"When you judge another, you do not define them, you define yourself." *Wayne Dyer*

The ego invented movies so it could watch itself.

Abstain. Don't live your life in the past lane.

"Remember one thing only: that it's you, nobody else, who determines your destiny and decides your fate. Nobody else can be alive for you; nor can you be alive for anybody else." *e. e. cummings*

Dreams come in metaphors so we can think about them, help make their meaning clear. That's what metaphors are for. The world is a disguised metaphor.

"Surround yourself only with people who are going to lift you higher." *Oprah Winfrey*

The ego mind and its manifestations, meaning the person we think we are, are always unconscious.

The ego mind is a work of fiction, created by a work of fiction, for a world of fiction.

"We are what we feel and perceive. If we are angry, we are the anger." *Thich Nhat Hanh*

"During our life together the issues of possessions, attachment and identification with the ego were in the forefront of our awareness and George was always quick to point out that in reality, there is no I, Me, or Mine." *Olivia Harrison, from the book, "I - ME - MINE"*

Krishnamurti Quotes

"Society is based on ambition and conflict, and almost everyone accepts this fact as inevitable. Real learning comes about when the competitive spirit has ceased."

"If you as a human being transform yourself, you affect the consciousness of the rest of the world."

"When you separate yourself by belief, nationality or tradition, it breeds violence. So one who is seeking to understand violence does not belong to any country, religion or political party, but is concerned with the total understanding of mankind."

"If there is to be any kind of social change, there must be a different kind of education so that children are not brought up to conform."

"Forget all you know about yourself; forget all you have ever thought about yourself; start as if you know nothing."

"The thing you fight, you become."

"The moment I am aware that I am aware, I'm not aware."

"Love will arise in your heart when you meet and observe people without judging them."

-

The ego desert mind is body karma. It cannot help but judge people by the color of their skin, the color of their hair, their education, or social standing, or what the body looks like they've have chosen to be in.

We can have a dream, or a thought, or vision, about something that hasn't happened yet, because there isn't anything that hasn't happened yet.

How can we tell when the ego-karma mind presses our button? Anytime we are unable to forgive, and without judgment - love and empathize "which what it seems" they have done to us, we have experienced our ego button. If we come to see them as "our buttons," and that they have nothing to do with the other person, or persons, then we will become determined to find a way, our own way, to accept that we press our own buttons, and then we will find a way to stop doing it. That's what this book is about.

The ego mind keeps running in place wondering when it will arrive at its destination.

"Fear is the mind-killer." *Frank Herbert - Dune*

The next time you're feeling bad about your life, your state of karma, watch "Marie's Story" on tubi, or wherever you can find it.

"Only the hand that erases can write the true thing."
Meister Eckhart

"Civilizations should be measured by the degree of diversity attained and the degree of unity retained."
W. H. Auden

"There are a group of people who are managing the world to their advantage and who just look to the rest of us as people who will buy their products and fund their salaries." *Jeremy Irons*

The only way out of this place is to remember you're not here, you've never been here, and will never be here.

"Karma is the universal law of cause and effect. You reap what you sow. You get what you earn. You are what you eat. If you give love, you get love. Revenge returns itself upon the avenger." *Mary Browne*

"To the world you might be one person, but to one person, you might be the world. Kindness is the golden chain by which our world is bound together." *Goethe*

"Yesterday I was clever, so I wanted to change the world. Today I am wise, so I am changing myself."
Rumi

"Be thine own palace, or the world's thy jail." \
John Donne

Waking up, going to sleep, both different versions of the same thing.

Dreams are an unwatched version of karma mind.

Karma gets up every morning well rested, convincing itself it has slept.

Ego-karma is fear.

Welcome to the karmic desert mind, birthplace of an ego psychological art form: Depressionism.

You must forget the past, because the past will never, can never, forget you.

"There is no was." *William Faulkner*

> In terror do we often flee
> from what would do us most good,
> as with open arms rush we
> to what would do us most harm.

"Never tell a child you have a soul. Teach him, you are a soul; you have a body." *George MacDonald*

"The secret of happiness, you see, is not found in seeking more, but in developing the capacity to enjoy less." *Socrates*

Karmic mind is a cause-and-effect domain.

Take time to Observe and Choose.

"It doesn't matter how old we are, the moment we depend on other peoples opinions for our validation, for our self-worth, we begin to die." *Source unknown*

The future is the past in karmic retrospect.

Invictus

"Out of the night that covers me,
Black as the pit from pole to pole,
I thank whatever gods may be
For my unconquerable soul."
William Ernest Henley

Ego is a double entendre with one meaning.

If we become used to music playing all the time, silence becomes distracting. If we become used to silence all the time music playing becomes distracting.

Pardon my interrupting dear reader,
but I seem to have forgot;
I started out, seems so long ago,
perhaps you remember, perhaps you know,
how much further to Camelot?

Music played, flowers grew again in places they grew in days of yore. New generations came unaware of hard earned lessons learned before.

"Knowing how to be solitary is central to the art of loving. When we can be alone, we can be with others without using them as a means of escape." *Bell Hooks*

Leaving karmic past behind is not easy, but we have no choice; it's already gone.

Stress isn't caused by life in the fast lane, or life in the slow lane, but by life in the past lane.

At some point it may occur to ask ourselves: Why have we made up this karma world?

Karma and peace will never rhyme.

"I found I had less and less to say, until finally, I became silent, and began to listen. I discovered in the silence, the voice of God." *Soren Kierkegaard*

"The true meaning of love one's neighbor is not that it is a command from God which we are to fulfill, but that through it and in it we meet God." *Martin Buber*

Some things must be done alone.

Given karmic unconscious is an ego extension of our individual unconscious mind, we are all to some extent; unconscious.

John Maynard Keynes Quotes

"The day is not far off when the economic problem will take the back seat where it belongs, and the arena of the heart and the head will be occupied or reoccupied, by our real problems, problems of life, of human relations, of creation, behavior and religion."

"The decadent international but individualistic capitalism in the hands of which we found ourselves after the *war is not a success. It is not intelligent. It is not beautiful. It is not just. It is not virtuous. And it doesn't deliver the goods." *WW2

"The political problem of mankind is to combine three things: economic efficiency, social justice and individual liberty."

"The social object of skilled investment should be to defeat the dark forces of time and ignorance which envelope our future."

"The difficulty lies not so much in developing new ideas as in escaping from old ones."

-

Creating the meaningless with the meaningless is karma's idea of meaning.

"Parents can only give good advice or put them on the right paths, but the final forming of a person's character lies in their own hands." *Anne Frank*

Choose to see differently now, right now! There is, nor will ever be, any other time to declare your freedom.

"They loved each other, not driven by necessity, by the "blaze of passion" often falsely ascribed to love. They loved each other because everything around them willed it, the trees and the clouds and the sky over their heads and the earth under their feet." *Boris Pasternak, From Doctor Zhivago*

Karma mind is the pursuit of pursuit.

"We are neurotic when we are not what God meant us to be." *Marie-Louise von Franz*

"The best things cannot be told because they transcend thought. The second best are misunderstood because they are the thoughts that are supposed to refer to that which cannot be thought about. The third best is what we talk about." *Joseph Campbell*

"Spiritual practice is not what you are doing, it is what you are thinking. It is with the mind we do everything. All of your problems would solve themselves if you were regular in your meditation." *Swami Satchidananda*

"Fear is only as strong as your avoidance of it. The greater your reluctance to see fear, to accept it, to embrace it, the more power you allow it. At times of giant steps in the souls evolutionary expansion there are moments of great insecurity." *Emanuel's Book, Book 1*

"Wherever we go, we bring our mind with us, so the world we see is subjective, our own predisposition conditions our impression of all events." *Carl Jung*

Memories both of so called good and fade, back to where they came, love never. But what is love? Love is absence of all memories but one.

"Trials are but lessons that you failed to learn presented once again, so where you made a faulty choice before you now can make a better one, and thus escape all pain that what you chose before has brought to you." *A Course In Miracles*

Ego-karmic mind gives names to all psychological and physical diseases it creates, then begins finding solutions.

Sometimes we can become so enamored of digging ourselves out of a psychological hole, we use it as a defense mechanism to forget why we're digging.

Beginnings are preferable to no beginnings at all.

To attempt and fail is to succeed.

Riding An Unknown Train

Riding an unknown train, just passing through,
just trying to make-do.
A stranger sitting with me?
Who is he? I don't know,
reading some book, cover letters in gold.

Stations passing by, sometimes I think I know why.
Incessant eyes looking through my windows,
seeing tired soldiers, still fighting on,
like ego robot drones, unconscious schizos,
behaving unconscious gung-ho's,
hiding from psychological no show's.
I see stations of the bourgeoisie,
marking the cost, the double cross.

I think I see me
in the window's reflection — wait:
I couldn't tell, was that my face?

I need to ask someone, but who would know?
For a moment there I couldn't recall my name
As I was just passing through, just passing through
on this unknown train.

"Parents can only give good advice or put them on the right paths, but the final forming of a person's character lies in their own hands." *Anne Frank*

"Not all those who wander are lost." *J.R.R. Tolkien, The Fellowship of the Ring*

> "The writing's on the wall brother
> Your life is in your hands
> It's up to you to see the writing's on the wall"
> *"Writings On The Wall," George Harrison*

"It's being here now that's important. There's no past and there's no future. Time is a very misleading thing. All there is ever, is the now. We can gain experience from the past, but we can't relive it; and we can hope for the future, but we don't know if there is one." *George Harrison*

There comes a time on our spiritual journey when we realize we have made progress, and we become very conscious of the danger involved in the *karmic pull* of wanting to go back. Then we do our best, usually it's one step forward, two steps back, something like that.

The more uncertainty and divisiveness in the world, or in our mind, the more sex may be used a tranquilizer. And then, the focus of our relationships is on the "sex itself," each person becoming an "object." Sex becomes the goal, the people involved secondary. This reiterates the *ego's ultimatum* to deny that we are spiritual beings, who are having a human experience.

"We had thought that we were human beings making a spiritual journey; it may be truer to say that we are spiritual beings making a human journey."
Pierre Teilhard de Chardin

Ego mind talks to itself, teaching itself what it already knows, believing it's learned something new.

"It may be that when we no longer know what to do, we have come to our real work, and that when we no longer know which way to go, we have begun our real journey." *Wendell Berry*

We make up a myth about someone in our mind, and when they don't live up to it, we blame them.

"If the only tool you have is a hammer, it is tempting to treat everything as if it were a nail." *Abraham Maslow*

Karmic ego mind programs itself to go backwards, then convinces it self it is going forward. Because of this self caused delusion it's always in a state of confusion, even when appearing not to be.

Memory and history, those are all learning skills we have taught ourselves, so we can remember our memory and our history.

Even peace has an opposite, war. The only thing without an opposite is love. Love is: seeing all people, all things, everything, absent of judgment.

Origin Of The Universe

"According to the early scriptures, the Buddha himself never directly answered questions put to him about the *origin of the universe.* In a famous simile, the Buddha referred to the person who asks such questions as a man wounded by a poisoned arrow. Instead of letting the surgeon pull the arrow out, the injured man insists first on discovering the caste, name, and clan of the man who shot the arrow; whether he is dark, brown, or fair; whether he lives in a village, town, or city; whether the bow used was a longbow or a crossbow; whether the bowstring was fiber, reed, hemp, sinew, or bark; whether the arrow shaft was of wild or cultivated wood; and so forth." *Source Unknown*

-

"My hope and wish is that one day, formal education will pay attention to what I call "education of the heart." Just as we take for granted the need to acquire proficiency in the basic academic subjects, I am hopeful that a time will come when we can take it for granted that children will learn, as part of the curriculum, the indispensability of inner values: love, compassion, justice, and forgiveness." *Dalai Lama*

-

Eastern spiritual psychology says there's a way to psychologically leave the 'everyday life frenzy' created by the karmic past buried in our mind. There is no one way, there are many, we each have to find one that works for us. It all depends on our cup of tea. Original/Spiritual existence is where there is no space between anything, yet are none encumbered.

Love is not related to the brain, or anything physical.

"Mindfulness is the art of experiencing the nonexistence of the past and the future."
Mokokoma Mokhonoana

"Dear girl, it will be a very long road if you spend more time looking backwards than forward."
Som*an Chainani, The Last Ever After*

Your ego is expressed when the light has turned red, and you hurriedly try to beat that yellow through the intersection.

"The geographical pilgrimage is the symbolic acting out of an inner journey. The inner journey is the interpolation of the meanings and signs of the outer pilgrimage. One can have one without the other. It is best to have both." *Thomas Merton*

Ego mind only sees through the past. And in that seeing, creates its future . . . like a rolling stone.

Organic is more than a table set, it's a mind set.

"Whether describing a king, an assassin, a thief, an honest man, a prostitute, a nun, a young girl, or a stall-holder in a market, it is always ourselves we are describing." *Guy de Maupassant*

"Wherever we go we bring our mind with us, so the world we see is subjective. Our predisposition conditions our impression of all events. Even if we were in Heaven, we wouldn't be able to see it, if there is hell in our mind." *Carl Jung*

Ego mind invented competition.

"All negativity is caused by an accumulation of psychological time and denial of the present."
Eckhart Tolle, The Power of Now

Years ago, after I lost my job, my best friend kept reminding me that I said nothing in this world was real. I see now I missed the point about the world not being real. We cannot deny that we think we live in the physical world, and that we need jobs to earn money to support our selves. We should ask, why are we here? What is our life for?

Nothing you see, or experience, or feel has any meaning except the that which you give it. There are only two meanings possible, regardless of the person, the situation, or the relationship: peace or conflict.

When someone presses your button, you found your karma.

Understanding what love is, involves a consciously sought after progressive realization of inter-dependent origination.

"When Is It Time To Leave A Painful Relationship?"

"When is it time to drop a hot pot?"
Swami Satchidananda

"Through violence you may solve one problem, but you sow the seeds for another." *Dalai Lama*

Today as always, the historically conditioned ego-karma mind is at war, its own inner war. The inner war now is, as it always has been, the loving need for an accepted psychological awareness of global inter-dependence; that is to say, accepting all the worlds people are mutual landlords in a shared climate house, a house called Earth.

"We are forlorn like children, experienced like old men, we are crude and sorrowful and superficial—I believe we are lost." *Erich Maria Remarque*

Another word for ego is conflict. Another word for conflict is war. The ego and its created assistant, the brain, laid siege to Ukraine.

"Men make war to get attention. All killing is an expression of self-hate." *Alice Walker*

The historically programmed ego mind is pushed to the wall to control what it's afraid of. And it is afraid of everything, including itself. So then, what does it do when it gets to the wall?

Ego mind is a narcissist that doesn't love itself, and despises itself for it.

A habit is a sub-personality to which we have given autonomy.

"All terms are potentially controversial, and those who see controversy will find it. Yet those who seek clarification will find it as well." *A Course In Miracles*

Ego-kamra mind thinking is like playing ping-pong with yourself, hoping to finally win.

I've become more patient lately. I've found things come faster that way.

"Give me love, Give me love
Give me peace on earth
Give me light, Give me life
Keep me free from birth
Trying to, touch and reach you with
Heart and soul"
George Harrison, from the song, "Give Me Love"

You can't save someone who's drowning if they think they're swimming.

Narcissism is another word for fear. Ego narcissism says to itself: I can't trust anyone to love me, so I'll just love myself, because no one can do it better.

The ego is a mask hiding a spiritual pandemic.

Hope and faith went for a swim. Faith learned to swim before diving in.

Karma creates buttons. Ego creates karma.

Karmic mind loves but itself, but knows not love.

Memory is a skill we have taught ourselves not to forget.

We shouldn't worry about what may happen in the future, but we should prepare. How to prepare and what to prepare for is the question.

"The sight of a child…will arouse certain longings in adult, civilized persons — longings which relate to the unfulfilled desires and needs of those parts of the personality which have been blotted out of the total picture in favor of the adapted persona." *Carl Jung*

Fear is a reflection of the unconscious mind watching itself.

"Spiritual practice is not what you are doing, it is what you are thinking. It is with the mind that we do everything." *Swami Satchidananda*

The right method for the wrong person, is the wrong method.

Ego mind is a lawyers dodge.

Pain

"If God is real, there is no pain. If pain is real, there is no God." *A Course In Miracles*

Meditation is thought. Whatever you're thinking about you're meditating on, and believing you are that.

The ego invented vacations to trick itself into thinking it could get away for a while.

Some people can predict the future because it's already happened.

After all is said and done cause-and-effect are one.

The ego is psychological cold war.

The law of karma is infallible; so every thing that has never happened, has already happened. When the student is ready the teacher, that has always been there, will appear to appear.

We are more afraid of solitude than anything else, afraid of what we might become aware of in ourselves.

"When I find myself in times of trouble, Mother Mary comes to me, speaking words of wisdom, let it be."
Beatles, "Let It Be"

We can be good at keeping secrets from ourselves.

"Ego Mind Werewolf Of Moscow"
Inspired by Warren Zevon's "Werewolves Of London"

I saw a ego-karmic werewolf,
with a war menu in his hand,
he was looking for a place
the Russian war machine could command.

He's stir-crazed, he's insane,
why he even invaded a democratic free Ukraine!
Look, he's selling oil and gas to Beijing and Berlin,
howling around the free worlds door!

Ego-karmic mind werewolf of Moscow;
free world better not let him in,
or the free world life we knew is through.
Ah-hoooooooo!

Poverty has a purpose. Mother Teresa showed it to us.

People ask me, teaching all the stuff in this book, how
do I feel in my practical everyday life, as I continue
my spiritual search. For example, how do I feel when I
get up in the morning, and have to face everyday
button difficulties? Well, I just get up, get dressed, go
to my car, open my trunk, and go to work.

Ego mind is psychological coma-karma.

"Anger is an acid that can do more harm to the vessel in which it is stored than to anything on which it is poured." *Mark Twain - quoted from Psychology Today*

Ego-karma mind is "memorizing politics of ancient history" *From the song "My Back Pages," Bob Dylan*

"We love to learn we're not alone."
Inspired by the movie "Shadowlands"

"You cannot swim for new horizons until you have courage to lose sight of the shore." *Author unknown*

We are controlled by sub-personalities of which we are hardly aware. We meet them in our dreams.

"Goodbyes are only for those who love with their eyes. Because for those who love with heart and soul there is no such thing as separation." *Rumi*

When the student is ready the ego appears.

Difficulty sleeping is incorrectly named; it should be called ego-somnia.

"Peace does not mean to be in a place where there is no noise, trouble or hard work. It means to be in the midst of those things and still be calm in your heart."
A quote from a cup I bought.

Stress is like a car still going down the street while parked.

Ego mind loves only itself. But ego mind knows not of love.

If too many people become upscale, the ego mind will invent upper-upscale!

Only in growing old can we fully experience what it feels like being young, as well as the benefits accrued to both.

Time passes slowly when one is in a hurry.

We can learn to see other's egos as our own.

War and peace are opposites. Peace has no opposite.

Heaven is a place where everyone is the same but with a different Light.

Fear is the unconscious mind aware of itself.

"Why do you want to persecute yourself with the question of where it all comes from and where it is leading? You well know you are in a period of transition and want nothing more than to be transformed." *Rainer Maria Rilke, From "Letters To A Young Poet."*

"What I am looking for is not out there, it is in me."
Helen Keller

"If you want to be creative, stay in part a child, with the creativity and invention that characterizes children before they are deformed by adult society." *Jean Piaget*

In spiritual practice if we try too hard the ego mind is involved. If we don't try hard enough, the ego mind is involved.

"Die the death of the ego and be reborn spiritually even in this very life." *Swami Prahavananda*

Chess is an ego mind game where one tries to think of every possible move which has already happened, before, and after it happened.

"All the greatest and most important problems of life are fundamentally not solvable. They can never be solved, but only outgrown." Carl Jung

Ego mind doesn't like to remember that it has nothing to remember.

Seeing with ego is like wearing glasses with the wrong prescription.

Meditation is hatha yoga for the mind.

Take time to Observe and Choose.

I will wake remembering,
You, there be beside me,
on the Yin/Yang bench
where you've been waiting.

You'll say let's go walking amidst the meadow,
everyone knows you're coming.
And so holding hands, once more will we go.

Ego mind: It's what you feel like when you get a
parking ticket and don't own a car.

"Your willingness to look at your darkness is what
empowers you to change." *Iyanla Vanzant*

Self doubt is merciless.

We are all karmaholics.

Ego causes its own insurrection and looks outside
itself for those responsible.

The ego world is a construction zone, always in need
of repair.

Ego-karma minds *only* goal is to avoid the emptiness,
the experience, the falsity, of its perceived loss.

Ego invented the symbols "King and Queen, " so it
could worship at its own throne.

From her book about WWI,
"Testament Of Youth,"
Vera Brittain

"And at last I had come to believe that, although men did change slowly, and left the evidence of their progressive modifications in statutes and treaties, no change would come soon enough to save the next generation from the grief and ruin that has engulfed my own so long as the world that I knew endured — the world of haves and have nots; of owners and owned; of rich and poor; of Great Powers and little nations, always at the mercy of the wealthy and strong; of influential persons whose interests were served by war, and who had sufficient authority to compel politicians to participate on behalf of a few, the wholesale destruction of millions."

Vera was only eighteen, "a child" with life hardly begun, in 1917 WWI broke out in Europe. As a result of the fighting, Vera lost her brother, her best friend, and her fiancé, each killed in that war. Sixteen years later, at age thirty-four, with two young children of her own, Vera wrote "for us" all about her life-changing experiences as a nurse during WW1 in her book, "Testament of Youth," which became a movie in 2014. You might want to watch it dear reader. Vera passed in 1977, sixty years after the start of WW1 at age 76. We can be certain, beyond doubt, that Vera would both, believingly and disbelievingly, watch as ego-karmic past history repeated its self, cleverly disguised as WWII.

The official next half of karma life begins when ego puberty-personality encounters the every day reality of others.

A physical pandemic is ego mind gone ballistic.

The ego is a comedian without a sense of humor, that only laughs at its own jokes.

Ego always plans ahead by looking back.

Ego is an escape hatch leading back in.

Being physically naked and psychologically naked with another are as different as hot water and ice.

There comes a time when your ego mind ceiling meets your ego mind floor, and you can't take it anymore. Emboldened by noose necessity, without concern for outcome, or income, you bolt for the door.

Sooner or later, for better or worse, all of us little children grow up. That's how things work around here.

When will we human beings grow tired of watching horror movies, war movies, any movies that project violence, physical or psychological, of any kind?

The ego is a no-show that showed up.

Satchidananda gave a word of advice, Mantra.

Whatever you're thinking about you're praying for.

Prayer is continuous.

If there's no end in sight, you're looking in the wrong direction.

Sex and love are not related. Sex is physical. Love is not.

Without faith and love prayer is a chair without legs.

Ego desert mind is authoritarianism.

Chooser mind is the place in our mind free of karma. It is the place that never left Spiritual Mind. For this reason it can choose to see our ego-karma mind with Spiritual vision, and with sustained practice, release it.

The ego is a mispelled word in a dictionary that doesn't exist. And dats dat.

When the world has taught us enough, we will willing let go of all the world has taught us.

If I only knew then what I know now, said the karmic butcher to the cow. The cow at a loss for words said: "Moooo."

"Mankind's greatest gift, also its greatest curse, is that we have free choice. We can make our choices built from love or from fear." *Elisabeth Kübler-Ross*

"There are two days in the year that we cannot do anything, yesterday and tomorrow." *Mahatma Gandhi*

If we can, even for a moment, conceive of, even try to conceive of the meaning of the Watcher/Chooser Mind, the ego-karma mind watcher, it means it is awake in us! Its presence has become conscious. If it wasn't we couldn't think about it. We have begun.

"One religion, like a single type of food, cannot satisfy everybody." *Dalai Lama from his book "In My Own Words"*

Karma is another word for unconscious. Unconscious is another word for ego. Ego is another word for fear.

Karma plays no favorites.

"This whole creation is essentially subjective, and the dream is the theater where the dreamer is at once: scene, actor, prompter, stage manager, author, audience, and critic." *Carl Jung*

"Everything depends on inner change; when this has taken place, then, and only then does the world change." *Martin Buber*

Ego mind invented success so it could fail.

With every thought we have you/we have a chance to *choose* to free ourself from "our" self created karma.

Karma is thought recycling, going on all the time, even as we sleep.

"War is only a cowardly escape from the problems of peace." *Thomas Mann*

"As human beings, our greatness lies not so much in being able to remake the world, that is the myth of the atomic age, as in being able to remake ourselves. Be the change you want to see in the world." *Mahatma Gandhi*

Dalai Lama: "Violence is never good, every result be it good or bad, it had a cause." "Nonviolence takes a long time." *From the movie "Kundun"*

"Who creates war? The bombs don't drop by themselves. It is the people behind them, the human minds that create war. All the wars are in the human mind." *Swami Satchidananda, Integral Yoga Magazine.org. August 2022*

"Each one of us has our own evolution of life, and each one of us goes through different tests which are unique and challenging. But certain things are common. And we do learn things from each other's experience. On a spiritual journey, we all have the same destination." *A. R. Rahman*

"The only journey is the one within." *Rainer Maria Rilke*

Karma is in the eyes of the beholder.

Karma is a foretold conclusion of a foreboding future.

Artificial intelligence is a psychological personality we think we have.

Being practical about your karma means going to the dentist for cavities, having convinced yourself you have teeth. And not forgetting to floss. 😊

Karma is not only blowing in the wind, karma is the wind.

Karma mind is the only problem we have. Until we realize that, we will try to solve our problems with karma mind, the mind that created the problems.

Everything historically learned is same form of karma.

We who think we are here, are karmic projections of our fragmented ego inventions.

> I'll get my nuclear football,
> you get yours.
> Try to go over my goal line,
> I'll try to go over yours.
> We'll keep on playing until somebody scores.

Think of what your life would be like if you had been walking backwards all the time, but thought you were walking forwards. That is what karma has us doing.

We make ourselves so tired we can't even fall asleep.

The historical mind loves to analyze itself, write great revered books about itself, and give talks about itself.

If we don't make up our mind, ego mind will make it up for us.

The ego is a one way street, going both ways in the same direction, at the same time.

No one has ever taken a breath when it isn't now.

Where is your karma now, unless you choose to bring it with you.

Has there ever been,
in any country, at any time in history,
a system of government *that hasn't produced conflict?*
The problem is not government,
or some legislations voted verdict enshrined.
The problem is the cause of all conflict:
the unwatched mind.

Karma is a desert. Flower's can't grow in a desert.

Mantra is a feather duster for karmic mind.

Karmic mind loves but itself. But karmic mind knows not how to love.

I didn't make my bed this morning and didn't feel guilty. I must be making spiritual progress!

Karma is everything remembered that never happened.

The ego mind is impermanent spiritual dementia.

War is an ego mind sub-personality.

Whatever you repress you become. Whatever you first accept, and then choose to let go of, you become.

Ego mind doesn't care about you.

This book is about finding out how to find peace of mind. But first we have to discover we have lost it.

What is karma? Karma is forgetting you're a spiritual being having a human experience.

Karma is *consciously* overlooking the fact that you are a non-physical being having a physical experience.

Spiritual Mind says you can't take it with you. Ego mind says, if I can't take it with me, I'll come back and get it.

"The spiritual journey is one of continuous learning and purification. When you know this, you become humble." *Sogyal Rinpoche*

"Just by the very nature of our birth, we are on the spiritual journey." *Thomas Keating*

Karma is what never happened happening again.

We're karma-tose until we're not.

Karma and liberty will never rhyme.

Karma is *continuous* psychological conflict, an unconscious war of unknowing revenge against itself.

The body is a tattoo on an ego-karma mind that doesn't exist.

"The spiritual journey is individual, highly personal. It can't be organized or regulated. It isn't true that everyone should follow one path. Listen to your own truth." *Ram Dass*

Every entrance has an exit, except one.

Courage never grows old on its often wearisome's long walk home.

"To have peace, teach peace to learn it." *A Course In Miracles*

If you feel like your boomerang won't come back, you've found your ego.

There's only one reason we can have a splitting headache. We have a split mind.

You can't keep secrets from the unconscious mind.

Chose peace. Choose again. Choose again.

Karma is a way back to where you've never been.

Karma is a place you've never been to, getting there and saying: it's great to be back again.

Old karmic habits are hard to break, especially the ones we don't know we have.

The ego mind and its manifestations, meaning the person we think we are, are always more or less unconscious.

"We kill to eat, we kill to live, and what we kill is killing us." *Swami Satchidananda*

Never lock the door to your heart. But think twice, twice, and twice again, who you give the key to.

"Remember: It's you and nobody else who determines your destiny and decides your fate.

"Nobody else can be alive for you; nor can you be alive for anybody else." *E. E. Cummings*

Dreams come in metaphors so we can think about them, help make their meaning clear. That's what metaphors are for. The world is a disguised karmic metaphor.

Tomorrow is a continuous consequence of yesterday in the unwatched karmic mind, seasons come, seasons go, weather is the only constant. Dress accordingly.

We can't have a dream about something that's never happened before, because there isn't anything that hasn't happened before.

"There's always the next big thing." *Ruth Rudy*

The ego is so self centered, so narcissistic, that it invented movies so it could watch itself, and give itself awards for watching.

"We are what we feel and perceive. If we are angry, we are the anger." *Thich Nhat Hanh*

Ego mind invented a type of karma it named chaos to prove it could start, control and solve the problem.

Ego mind has all its ducks in a row. And though we each think we're different, we all quack the same way.

We should ask why was there, why does there continue to be a need for Mother Theresa?

"What the mind is trying to figure out the heart already knows." *Adapted, Emmanuel's Book - Book One*

Your particular ego-karma was, and is a choice you consciously or unconsciously made, and are making even as you read this. At every moment of our life we are determining the meaning of our life.

"Civilizations should be measured by the degree of diversity attained and the degree of unity retained."
W. H. Auden

The only way out of this place is to remember you're not here.

"Be thine own palace, or the world's thy jail."
John Donne

Meditation; if it's too difficult for you to do, just spend some time each day thinking or reading about spiritual things, desire for more will grow.

Karma is a sold out concert with nobody there.

"There is no was." *William Faulkner*

"I'm starting with the man in the mirror
I'm asking him to change his ways
And no message could have been any clearer
If you want to make the world a better place
Take a look at yourself, and then make a change"

Michael Jackson, from his song, "Man In The Mirror

"We must be willing to let go of the life we planned, so as to have the life that is waiting for us." *Joseph Campbell*

"You must change your mind, not your behavior, and this is a matter of willingness." *Course In Miracles.*

"Change will not come if we wait for some other person, or if we wait for some other time. We are the ones we've been waiting for. We are the change that we seek." *Barack Obama*

Everyone thinks of changing the world, but no one thinks of changing himself." *Leo Tolstoy*

"Education is the most powerful weapon which you can use to change the world." *Nelson Mandela*

"Therefore, dear Sir, love your solitude and try to sing out with the pain it causes you."
Rainer Maria Rilke, "Letters to a Young Poet"

"Only the hand that erases can write the true thing."
Meister Eckhart

"I have accepted fear as part of life – specifically the fear of change... I have gone ahead despite the pounding in the heart that says: turn back" *Erica Jong*

Experience isn't something you learn, it's something you earn.

"Taking a new step, uttering a new word, is what people fear most." *Fyodor Dostoevsky, Crime and Punishment*

"Some changes look negative on the surface but you will soon realize that space is being created in your life for something new to emerge." *Eckhart Tolle*

"Change the way you look at things and the things you look at change." *Wayne W. Dyer*

Revenge is ego-karmic mind chess for one.

"We are taught you must blame your father, your sisters, your brothers, the school, the teachers - but never blame yourself. It's never your fault. But it's always your fault, because if you wanted to change you're the one who has got to change."
Katharine Hepburn, Me: Stories of My Life

"To change something, build a new model that makes the existing model obsolete." *Buckminster Fuller*

"The secret of happiness, you see, is not found in seeking more, but in developing the capacity to enjoy less." *Socrates*

"There's as many atoms in a single molecule of your DNA as there are stars in the typical galaxy. We are, each of us, a little universe." *Neil deGrasse Tyson, Cosmos*

An unexpected - gone almost the instant it came - burst of anger *towards another person,* reveals only a "microscopic" amount *of ones own,* repressed, and purposefully forgotten psychological PAIN. Ego buried it below conscious awareness in karma mind so long ago so, it seemed forgotten. SUDDENLY something pushed the past ego-karma button! And, just as a living person would - remembering that long ago victimized pain, karma mind SCREAMED in rage, complaining it had been abandoned, unloved. And . . . refusing responsibility: *Blamed the one screamed at.*

-

Psychological helpers, come in many forms, some may even appear to cause us great anger and despair, but if seen with spiritual vision, they can help us to see that *psychologically,* there are no victims or victimizers

If we become used to music playing all the time, silence becomes distracting. If we become used to silence all the time music becomes distracting.

"Knowing how to be solitary is central to the art of loving. When we can be alone, we can be with others without using them as a means of escape." *Bell Hooks*

At some point it may occur to ask ourselves: Why have we made up this world of karma?

"I found I had less and less to say, until finally, I became silent, and began to listen. I discovered in the silence, the voice of God." *Soren Kierkegaard*

"The true meaning of love one's neighbor is not that it is a command from God which we are to fulfill, but that through it, and in it, we meet God." *Martin Buber*

To study neurology separate from psychology is like to trying to eat with your mouth closed.

Now is the time that never was! Observe the moment, live for the Awareness, only for its unchanging love and kindness. Find a way to ask help only for this, until it becomes the only thing you want.

Given that the karmic unconscious is an ego extension of our unconscious mind, with a name we've given our self, we are all unconscious

"Parents can only give good advice or put them on the right paths, but the final forming of a person's character lies in their own hands." *Anne Frank*

"Let us hope that we are all preceded in this world by a love story." *From the movie "Sweet Land"*

"As I walked out the door toward the gate that would lead to my freedom, I knew if I didn't leave my bitterness and hatred behind, I'd still be in prison."
Nelson Mandela

"When you begin to see that your enemy is suffering, that is the beginning of insight."
Thich Nhat Hanh, Peace Is Every Step

Physical bodies can never join to love each other.
because love is only of the mind. Doing the best we
can at the time, we can choose to be aware of this.

Peaceheart Road

Peaceheart road,
It could be a long way back,
shouldn't we should start today?

Shouldn't we start today
deciphering the code,
heavens hollowed tender ode,
the final passageway back to
Peace Heart Road.

Spiritual boats on the water leave no trace of journeys
made, make no waves.

"All Together Now" let's sing a
George Harrison song of long ago,
anyone George has done will be apropos;
any one George has done, how about
"Here Comes The Sun?"

We human's made laws to assure justice is done. But
justice can be interpreted differently, Spiritual love
cannot. Law and justice are two different things.

"He who is not satisfied with a little is satisfied with
nothing." *Epicurus*

Every joy is in loving, every sadness in not having loved.

Never hold any head higher than your own.

The strong survive. The weak perish.The wise surrender.

Flower Power, it's the only power worth fighting for, and you can't fight for flower power.

The ego loves only itself. But the ego knows not how to love.

"The best way to predict your future is to create it." *Abraham Lincoln*

Does a fish see the water it lives in?

"When you want to hurry something, that means you no longer care about it and want to get on to other things." *Robert M. Pirsig, Zen and the Art of Motorcycle Maintenance*

There are only two types of people: Those who lead, and those who follow. And when we lead, nothing matters more than who we follow.

If sex is the main course desert won't satisfy.

After all is said and done cause-and-effect become one.

Revenge is self inflicting.

Relationships are a lot like driving in heavy traffic: If you crash into someone because you're following too close, don't blame them.

What if Cosmo, Hollywood, and all the others, the advertisers, decided highlighting big breasts was out, would women put them back in?

"No one is ever really taught by another; each of us has to teach himself. The external teacher offers only the suggestion, which arouses the internal teacher, who helps us to understand things." *Swami Vivekananda*

"I believe we have breaks because we need them. So my suggestion is that you take the break. Eat chocolate." *Donna Jo Napoli*

"Having courage does not mean that we are unafraid. Having courage and showing courage means we face our fears. We are able to say, 'I have fallen, but I will get up." *Maya Angelou*

"The denial of aging is unhealthy."
Emma Thompson, New York Times, May 2019

When will more of us seniors accept ourselves as we are now?

Whose love and approval do we still need? What are we running from, scared of ? Why do so many of us try to "look young," color our hair, face lift, botox, etc?

You know, if we can't accept ourselves, accept aging gracefully, how can we expect others to do the same?

Importantly: By not accepting ourselves as we age, we create a double bind - we both deny we're older, and so, unconsciously, sell those fearful ideas to those still young, telling them; beware - do not look or get old!

"During the past 30 years people from all the civilized countries of the earth have consulted me. Among all my patients in the second half of life, that is to say over 35, there has not been one who's problem in the last resort was not that of finding a religious outlook on life. This of course has nothing whatever to do with the particular creed or membership of the church."
Carl Jung passed in 1961

"When You Are Old"
William Butler Yeats

"When you are old and grey and full of sleep,
And nodding by the fire, take down this book,
And slowly read, and dream of the soft look
Your eyes had once, and of their shadows deep;

How many loved your moments of glad grace,
And loved your beauty with love false or true.
But one man loved the pilgrim soul in you,
And loved the sorrows of your changing face;

And bending down beside the glowing bars,
Murmur, a little sadly, how Love fled
And paced upon the mountains overhead
And hid his face amid a crowd of stars.

Perhaps they are not stars,
but rather openings in heaven
where the love of our lost ones pours through,
and shines down upon us
to let us know they are happy."

November 22, 1963

Warmhearted in the cold, far, far from Camelot,
waits time's response to a place time begot.

Twilight loved ones remote,
those innocent we knew, those we remember,
those who live on, live and let live,
forgive them that November.

Shall they too, at long last seem to be born again?
And freed from the chronicles of time,
the sacred alliance shall seem to return.

So dearest brothers and sisters,
should St. Crispin regarding whereabouts inquire,
I request forget me not, for I am lost and alone,
and oh so from home, far far from Camelot.

Beneath The Ruins

Beneath the ruins, the sentry resolute, sounds the call.
Donors, marionettes of themselves,
kiss and tell, then they sleep.
Yet relinquishing nothing, knowing not, they weep.

But sleep they do, thinking they live,
and live they do, beneath the ruins.

"Until you make the unconscious conscious, it will direct your life and you will call it fate." *Carl Jung*

"There's no coming to consciousness without pain." *Carl Jung*

With meditation nothing changes except how we perceive things. And with that all things change.

"A single rose can be my garden." *Leo Buscaglia*

"Each one has to find his peace from within. And peace to be real must be unaffected by outside circumstances." Mahatma Gandhi

"Meditation means creating a continual familiarity with a virtuous object in order to transform your mind. The journey is the destination." *Dalai Lama*

Long periods of meditation are not for everyone this time around. So what then shall one do?

"Science cannot solve the ultimate mystery of nature. And that is because, in the last analysis, we ourselves are a part of the mystery that we are trying to solve." *Max Planck*

"Morality cannot be legislated" *Martin Luthur King*

Even though it is an illusion the karmic material world can be used for the purpose for which it was meant.

"My love belongs to those who can see it." *George Harrison*

Karma is everything you remember that never happened.

The ego mind is a form of spiritual dementia.

"The great force of history comes from the fact that we carry it within us, are unconsciously controlled by it in many ways, and history is literally present in all that we do." *James A. Baldwin*

War mind set is an ego mind sub-personality that is always active, never ceasing, always enemy seeking.

Buddha Expressing the Four Noble Truths
"Know the sufferings although,
there is nothing to know.
Relinquish the causes of misery,
although there is nothing to relinquish.
Be earnest in cessation although,
there is nothing to cease.
Practice the means of cessation,
although there is nothing to practice."
From the Dalai Lama's first book after leaving Tibet in 1959, "My Land and My People." Paperback, page 204.

The spiritual journey is one of continuous learning and purification. When you know this, you become humble. *Sogyal Rinpoche*

"You spend so much of your life, basing your self on what you think other people think of you. Then you realize that may be one of the purposes of life is not to care." *Dustin Hoffman*

Karma mind is the pursuit of pursuit.

"Fear is only as strong as your avoidance of it. The greater your reluctance to see the fear, to accept it, and embrace it, the more power you allow it. At times of giant steps in the souls evolutionary expansion there are moments of great insecurity." *Emanuel's Book, Book 1*

"Wherever we go, we bring our mind with us, so the world we see is subjective, our own predisposition conditions our impression of all events." *Carl Jung*

Next time you need a person to blame for your stress, your buttons, call your name *out loud.*

"It may be that, when we no longer know what to do, we have come to our real work, and that when we no longer know which way to go, we have begun our real journey." *Wendell Berry*

"Dear girl, it will be a very long road if you spend more time looking backwards than forward."
Soman Chainani, The Last Ever After

Observe, Choose, oftentimes.

"To live in the eternal present there must be death to the past, to memory. There is freedom when the entire being, the superficial as well as the hidden, is purged of the past." *Most likely Alan Watts, I forget, tired of looking.*

"We had thought that we were human beings making a spiritual journey; it may be truer to say that we are spiritual beings making a human journey." *Pierre Teilhard de Chardian*

Karmic ego mind programs itself to go backwards, then convinces it self it is going forward. Because of this self caused delusion it's always in the state of confusion, even when appearing not to be.

"All great beginnings start in the dark, when the moon greets you to a new day at midnight." *Shannon L. Alder*

"Sometimes, reaching out and taking someone's hand is the beginning of a journey. At other times, it is allowing another to take yours." *Vera Nazarian, The Perpetual Calendar of Inspiration*

Karma resembles flashing red tail lights in the pouring rain storm, nearly impossible to see.

"The geographical pilgrimage is the symbolic acting out of an inner journey. The inner journey is the interpolation of the meanings and signs of the outer pilgrimage. One can have one without the other. It is best to have both." *Thomas Merton*

Waking up, going to sleep are both different versions
of the same thing.

Eyes wide he said he heard a silent voice say:
I'll stay with you when sharks come close to shore,
I'll stay with you when night wolves howl at your door,
I'll befriended you when friends you have no more,
I'll help you plow so harvest will always be sure.

"Be scared. You can't help that. But don't be afraid."
William Faulkner

I've become more patient lately. I've found things
come faster that way.

"Only the hand that erases can write the true thing."
Meister Eckhart

Ego is a double entendre with one meaning.

Ego-karma invented iPhone's so it could talk to itself,
send it self messages and video's, so it could always be
in touch with itself, so it could get scam calls, etc.

Some days I feel like an electric toothbrush
without a charger,
like an electric flosser without water,
like a barker without a bark,
like a person in a car
always looking for a place to park.

"There are only two emotions: love and fear. All positive emotions come from love, all negative emotions from fear.

From love flows happiness, contentment, peace, and joy. From fear comes anger, hate, anxiety and guilt.

It's true that there are only two primary emotions, love and fear. But it's more accurate to say that there is only love or fear, for we cannot feel these two emotions together, at exactly the same time. They're opposites. If we're in fear, we are not in a place of love. When we're in a place of love, we cannot be in a place of fear." *Elisabeth Kubler-Ross*

"You have your way. I have my way. As for the right way, the correct way, and the only way, it does not exist." *Friedrich Nietzsche*

The latest fashion is a way of hiding ourselves in who we want to think we are today. Fashion is fickle.

What is love?

Well, everyone has said what they think love is, what it feels like when they've experienced it, when they're in it, and when it goes away, so, I might as well, give it a try. Love is the *completed experience* of the complete absence of judgment, of sin, guilt, fear. the absence of good or bad, happy or sad, weak or strong, of winners or losers. I haven't experienced it yet, but I'm working on it. How about you?

"Remember, to hate, to be violent, is demeaning. It means you're afraid of the other side of the coin, to love and be loved." *James A. Baldwin*

"The greatest thing you ever learn how to love and be loved in return." *From the song "Nature Boy," Nat King Cole*

"The more you struggle to live, the less you live. Give up the notion that you must be sure of what you are doing. Instead, surrender to what is real within you, for that alone is sure, you are above everything distressing." *Baruch Spinoza*

The Only Hope

Guarded hellos in a world
of memorized goodbyes.

Love not recognized between noble tears,
diminished by time, but not by heart.
Our bond, the only law,
love the only honor.

Our tears pure, our love fragile,
yet strong of itself.
Spiritual Mind is love.
Love is the only hope.

J.D. Salinger Quotes

"I'm just sick of ego, ego, ego. My own and everybody else's. I'm sick of everybody that wants to get somewhere, do something distinguished and all, be somebody interesting. It's disgusting."

"Among other things, you'll find that you're not the first person who was ever confused and frightened and even sickened by human behavior. You're by no means alone on that score, you'll be excited and stimulated to know. Many, many men have been just as troubled morally and spiritually as you are right now."

"That's all I do all day. I'd just be the catcher in the rye and all. I know it's crazy, but that's the only thing I'd really like to be."

"An artist's only concern is to shoot for some kind of perfection, and on his own terms, not anyone else's."

"Know your true measurements and dress your mind accordingly"

"One day a long time from now you'll cease to care anymore whom you please or what anybody has to say about you. That's when you'll finally produce the work you're capable of."

"If a body catch a body coming through the rye."

-

Ego mind loves only itself. But ego mind knows nothing of love.

Marriage is a karmic created idea. How can what was never separated believe it must be joined?

Only in growing old can we fully experience what it feels like being young, as well as benefits accrued to both.

Time passes slowly when one is in a hurry.

The only thing to know about your unconscious mind is: *it's unconscious,* and is directing your behavior.

The historically programmed ego mind is pushed to the wall to control what it's afraid of. And it is afraid of everything, including itself. So then, what does it do when it gets to the wall?

"All the greatest and most important problems of life are fundamentally not solvable. They can never be solved, but only outgrown." *Carl Jung*

> "I have seen my life belongs to me,
> My love belongs to who can see it."
> *From George Harrison's song "Who Can See It"*

Fear is a reflection of the unconscious mind watching itself.

The karmic mind is a night and day thought system.

You can try to love everyone else, to avoid loving yourself.

Eckhart Tolle said in a video that if we completely understood the first lesson of a A Course In Miracles, we wouldn't need any other lessons: "Nothing I see means anything,"

Ego plans ahead by looking back.

"The only real danger that exists is men himself. He is the great danger and we are pitifully unaware of it. We know nothing of men. Far too little " *Carl Jung 1959*

Mrs. Pi came to visit most unexpectedly,
one bright and sunny day. So I made a place for her,
told her I was glad she came. Invited her to stay.

I told her Mr. Pi was welcome anytime, any day,
in fact, in anticipation, I made a place for him to stay!
Mr. Pi will be along soon Mrs. Pi did say,
But no need for you to be concerned about that.

Olivia, who normally is not very friendly,
Olivia's my cat . . . had one look at Mrs. Pi,
Came right over and sat in her lap.
And that it seems - was that.

For Raphaela

Hanging out near Commerce and Barrow, I walk those grand old West Village streets, straight and narrow.

Yet even here, those staccato siren whir and whir, ambulance sounds, **POUND AND POUND.** But silencing of familiar New York sounds can still be found near here, where on a fine wooden bench I sit, feeling felicities flowering powers of St. Luke's Garden flowers.

Ego mind is fearful of forgetting that it has nothing to remember.

Seeing with ego is like wearing contacts with the wrong prescription.

Ego mind is what you feel like when you get a parking ticket and you don't own a car.

Being physically naked and psychologically naked with someone, are as different as hot water and ice.

Inside every highly competitive, hard driving ego-karma adult, shrouded inside an unconscious lonely karma hiddenness, there lives a small frightened child, afraid of life, afraid of love, but mostly afraid of itself.

The ego is a no-show that showed up.

Ego-karma mind thoughts are continuously cumulative.

When I was perhaps five or six, I decided I would try to stay up to see Santa and his Reindeer passing across the moon, but I fell asleep, and gradually, grew up, and became to old to try again.

"Mankind's greatest gift, also its greatest curse, is that we have free choice. We can make our choices built from love or from fear." *Elisabeth Kübler-Ross*

"Life will give you whatever experience is most helpful for the evolution of your consciousness. How do you know this is the experience you need? Because this is the experience you are having at the moment."
Eckhart Tolle

Karma is another word for the unconscious mind.

Karma is in the eyes of the beholder.

The only proof needed to prove that karma is real, is that you think you're reading this.

Karma has a mind of its own, it's called the unconscious.

Capitalism is an ego invented economic system that lasted for centuries and centuries.

Artificial intelligence is a psychological personality we have consciously forgotten we think we have.

"And now here is my secret, a very simple secret: It is only with the heart that one can see rightly; what is essential is invisible to the eye." *Antoine de Saint-Exupéry*

"The secret of happiness, you see, is not found in seeking more, but in developing the capacity to enjoy less." *Socrates*

"Beware the barrenness of a busy life." *Socrates*

Living In The Material World

"Got a lot of work to do
Try to get a message through
And get back out of this material world"
George Harrison, from the song,
"Living In The Material World"

Ego-karma and the material/physical world are the same. They are the world *we seemed to begin to create and experience* when we had the thought that we could separate from Spiritual Mind.

Eastern spirirtual psychology teaches we cannot separate from Spirirtual Mind, from our Creator, we come from that. It's like our Mom and Dad, we can't change that they were our Mom and Dad.

But we have free will to <u>interpret</u> what we see, and we can misinterpret, *and believe we've have separated.* The moment we thought we separated, the domino karma cause-and-effect material world began. This means that everything that has ever happened, and everything that will ever will happen in the material world, has already happened.

Without in any way, denying we think we live in the every day physical world, knowing we must adjust our lives to that reality, we should at the same time, find to a way to remember: We are spiritual beings, who have *chosen* to have a human/physical/material world experience, yet, we must live everyday practical lives.

Interpretation

"All human knowledge
takes the form of interpretation."
Walter Benjamin

Dear reader, everything in this book is about Mr. Benjamin's quote. It means: We as ego-karma human beings, give everything we see, everything we experience, both in seeing ourselves and so called others, all the meaning it has for us. And what we see, what we experience, is based on our acculturated, historical, educated life. In other words, we give everything we see our interpretation of it, based on our past karma. We don't see things as they are, but as we see them based on our past. And so we make up the world we see. And we have made up our mind about how we're going to see it even before we see it.

-

I'm writing this for whoever happens to read it.

We are slowed down sound and light waves, a walking bundle of frequencies tuned into the cosmos. We are souls dressed up in sacred biochemical garments and our bodies are the instruments through which our souls play their music. *Albert Einstein*

Someday the latest and the greatest will be the oldest and the grayest. The shrewdest and the Buddhist, the biggest and the best . . . we will all die like all the rest.

The Checking Account Of Past Thoughts,
And Spiritual Mind

The unconscious ego-karma mind works like a checking account. We put thoughts into it, and like a checking account, we can't take any money, or any thoughts out, we haven't put in. And, because of cause and effect, every time we have a thought, we make another thought deposit, in this way, we perpetually are creating our unconscious *person-ality, the person we think we are,* which is a history account of thoughts.

This means we give everything going on in our lives - at the present moment - even with our life's continually changing circumstances - all the meaning it has for us, based on the past thoughts we've deposited in our unconscious mind checking account.

So, because of our past history and perpetual thought deposits, everything we think and evaluate, decisions we make about what to do in our lives *now,* are based on our past thinking. We are using the thoughts we deposited in the unconscious mind, since our youth, up until now - those same thoughts that got us into a problem situation we're in - we're using those past thought deposits to solve the very problem it created.

And, there is one thing we know for sure about the past; it doesn't exist anymore - except - in our unconscious, unwatched, ego-karma mind.

All addiction is a way of burying, or not looking at, our perceived spiritual emptiness. Ego is an addiction.

If you burn your bridges, keep your boat and make sure you know how to row.

The future lies waiting below the old cold psychological ego desert mind trenches of the past.

Karma is the only problem we have. But until we realize that, we will try not to find a way to solve that problem.

We are each karmic ego extensions, karmic ego projections, of our own fragmented ego inventions.

Karmic pain must be seen and healed first from the top down. Only then can it be healed from the bottom up,

Ego, the person we think we are, is afraid most of non-judgmental love of all, regardless of their worldly acts. Because with that kind of love, ego has to face its own judgement, as well as its own end.

Karma is inherently narcissistic, because all it can remember is itself.

Karma creates its future, the past, in another form.

Karma being an authoritarian version of itself, is always in fear *of it self.*

Karma has many versions, but only one source.

The historical mind loves to analyze itself.

If we don't make up our mind, ego mind will make it up for us - will make us up.

The ego is a one way street that goes both ways in the same direction.

Capitalism was necessary. So was kindergarten.

No one has ever taken a breath when it isn't now.

"You may believe that you are responsible for what you do, but not for what you think. The truth is you are responsible for what you think, because it is only at that level you can exercise choice. What you do comes from what you think." *A Course In Miracles*

Karma is felicity forgotten.

Has there ever been a system of government that has not produced conflict? The problem is not government, the problem is the unwatched mind.

"Your willingness to look at your darkness is what empowers you to change." *Iyanla Vanzant*

The karma house was burning down, still some people inside insisted on locking the doors.

Karma is a desert, find a way to leave.

Mantra is a feather duster for karmic mind.

Karmic mind loves but itself. But karmic mind knows not how to love.

I didn't make my bed this morning and didn't feel guilty. I must be making spiritual progress!

Karma is everything you remember that never happened.

Whatever you repress you become. Whatever you accept and then choose to let go of, you also become.

Ego mind doesn't care about you.

What is karma? Karma is forgetting you're a spiritual being having a human experience.

"Just by the very nature of our birth, we are on the spiritual journey." *Thomas Keating*

Ego-karma is continuous psychological conflict. It's an unconscious war of unaware revenge against itself.

Ego desert mind is an undercover form of self hate.

Button free mind is love.

It's possible for us to be psychologically lost for so long, that we forget we're lost. As a consequence, we experience being lost as normal.

All stress is repressed karmic fear.

The body is a tattoo on an ego desert mind that doesn't exist.

"Never tell a child 'you have a soul.' Teach him, you are a soul; you have a body." *George MacDonald*

"The spiritual journey is individual, highly personal. It can't be organized or regulated. It isn't true that everyone should follow one path. Listen to your own truth." *Ram Dass*

I knew my karmic life was at a tipping point when my GPS told me to check back because all the team members were busy helping other drivers.

Desert ego mind personalities come in three forms; melting, freezing, frozen.

Karma is an empty jet full of people thinking it's flying coast-to-coast.

Get up, try again, start again my weary friend. This have I spoken to myself many times on the mend.

You can't keep secrets from the unconscious mind.

There's only one reason we can have a splitting headache. We have a split mind.

If you feel like your boomerang won't come back, you've found your ego

Karma is a place you've never been to, getting there and saying: it's good to be back again.

Old karmic habits are hard to break, especially the ones we don't know we have, because they have us.

Anything you find helpful in this book use, anything you don't, into the garbage. Piece of cake.

To deny what is seen physically is lunacy, thinking it's real is psychological atrophy.

Karma is a sold out concert with nobody there.

"Civilizations should be measured by the degree of diversity attained and the degree of unity retained."
W. H. Auden

No one has ever taken a breath when it wasn't now.

Dreams come in metaphors so we can think about them, help make their meaning clear. That's what metaphors are for. The world is a disguised karmic metaphor.

The ego invented vacations to trick itself into thinking it could get away for a while.

Just like being an introvert, or an extrovert, war is another personality type of ego karma.

We can't have a dream about something that's never happened before, because there isn't anything that hasn't happened before in some way.

Your particular karma was, is, a choice, consciously chosen, and are choosing again, even as you read this. This also includes reading and finding this book.

Karma, based on cause-and-effect, is infallible.

If we cannot, forgive, and forgiving has nothing to do with the other person, we carry the disappointment, the pain, the anger, the hurt of our inability to forgive within us, and in that way harm only ourselves. The benefit of forgiveness is self experienced and has nothing to do with anyone but ourselves.

If we want to keep solving the world's problems we can do that using artificial intelligence, which created all the world's problems in the first place. So what we're doing is using the mind that created all the problems to solve all the problems. There is only one problem, there is only one solution.

Karmic-ego unconscious is an ego extension of our unconscious mind, along with a name it has given us.

All of us here, are more or less, unconscious

We're clowns without faces. Maybe someday we'll live in a world where no one locks their doors

We'll know how far we've dug ourselves in, when we realize how far we've dug ourselves out.

Sometimes cold feet keep you on your toes about things.

You must forget the past, for the past will cannot forget you.

Psychological helpers, come in many forms, some may even appear to cause us great anger and despair, they can help us to see there are no victims or victimizers spiritually speaking.

If we become used to music playing all the time, silence becomes distracting. If we become used to silence all the time music becomes distracting.

Stress is caused by self inflicted psychological novocain: by life in the past lane.

See that squirrel over there, hiding behind the tree,
looking so intently at you and me?
Do you ever wonder
what it is he thinks he sees?
What he thinks we are?
What he thinks are trees?

"Knowing how to be solitary is central to the art of loving. When we can be alone, we can be with others without using them as a means of escape." *Bell Hooks*

At some point it may occur to ask ourselves: Why have we made up this world of karma?

"The true meaning of love one's neighbor is not that it is a command from God which we are to fulfill, but that through it and in it we meet God." *Martin Buber*

Once-upon-time this all seemed real.

Namaste to each of you in all you do. Om Shanti.

Physical bodies can never join in loving each other, because love being of the mind isn't physical. Doing the best we can at the time, we can choose to be aware of this to help undo ego-karmic mind

Laws can be interpreted differently, love cannot.

The ego loves only itself, but knows not how to love.

Take a moment to Observe and Choose.

"If you do not tell the truth about yourself, you cannot tell it about other people." *Virginia Woolf*

Heaven calls its own,
yet are not all of heaven?
Heaven chooses its own,
so are not all chosen?

Yes,
but many choose not to listen,
and so the call becomes
complicated, theorized,
analyzed, formalized,
unheard, unanswered,
unrecognized.

"I dream of giving birth to a child who will ask, *Mother, what was war?*" *Eve Merria*

At night Observe what you've hidden in your dream closet. Observe the person the unconscious wants you to be. Then *choose "consciously"* what you want to be.

"I'd rather see the world through the words of the Beatles, and the Eagles, than Karl Marx." *Sandy Tenzer*

Who?

Who will come to save us?
We self made prisoners of
primitive psychologies,
participants of interest earning
financial dynasties.
Will it be real estate angels
with more bedrooms,
more square feet,
more bigger, better, best?

Will it be bankers in
unconscious smokescreen,
unaware of their own disguise?
How much longer will we wait?

We are old karmic pros,
not knowing we are lost,
lost in an educational malaise we revere,
lost in a diversionary intellectual debate,
still arguing over which One is the real one.
Who will come to save us?

Even though it is an illusion, the karmic material world can be used for the purpose for which it made.

"Meditation means creating a continual familiarity with a virtuous object in order to transform your mind. The journey is the destination." *Dalai Lama*

"Even if we transport all the bombs to the moon, the roots of war and the roots of bombs are still there, in our hearts and minds, and sooner or later we will make new bombs. To work for peace is to uproot war from ourselves and from the hearts of men and women. To prepare for war, to give millions of men and women the opportunity to practice killing day and night in their hearts, is to plant millions of seeds of violence, anger, frustration, and fear that will be passed on for generations to come. " *Thich Nhat Hanh, Living Buddha, Living Christ*

The only way out of here is remembering you've never been here.

Spiritual practice is not what you are doing, it is what you are thinking. It is with the mind that we do everything.

All of your problems would solve themselves if you were regular in your meditation." *Swami Satchidananda*

"Wherever we go, we bring our mind with us, so the world we see is subjective, our own predisposition conditions our impression of all events." *Carl Jung*

There comes a time on the spiritual journey when we know we have made progress, because we become *conscious* of the danger involved, of the devious karmic pull of wanting to go back, and knowing better, doing our best to not succumb.

Sometimes we can become so enamored of digging ourselves out of a psychological hole, as a defense we can forget why we were digging.

Ego mind talks to itself, teaching itself what it already knows, making believe it's something new.

Beginnings are preferable to no beginnings at all, and to attempt and fail is to succeed.

"It may be that when we no longer know what to do, we have come to our real work, and that when we no longer know which way to go, we have begun our real journey." *Wendell Berry*

"As I see it, you cannot avoid the consequences of the past, you need to go through it in order to be free from it. It comes not as a punishment. It's to help you see what you didn't see before." *Amrit Desai*

Being practical about your karma means going to the dentist for cavities, having convinced yourself you have teeth. And not forgetting to floss.

"You know we've got to find a way
To bring some lovin' here today"
Words from "What's Going On," Marvin Gaye

"The timeless in you is aware of life's timelessness. And knows that yesterday is but today's memory and tomorrow is today's dream." *Khalil Gibran, The Prophet*

Ego-karma mind is the greatest story never told. Karma has an opposite: love. Love has no opposite.

Love without peace is impossible. Peace without love is impossible.

Karma is like eating donuts for what's in the middle

Karma is chess for one.

Ego karmic mind gives names to all the psychological and physical diseases it has created, and then begins finding solutions to have them eliminated.

"Distance yourself from the people that you don't want to become." *Shane Parish*

"There is not a heart that exists in your human world that, if it were assured of safety, would not open instantly. It is all an issue of fear. You fear to love an imperfect world." *Emanuel's Book, Book One*

All the world's problems originate in the mind, and there is no psychological vaccine for karmic epidemics that has yet been fully recognized, and thus put into effect.

The difference between ego mind and zoo animals is: ego mind will never acknowledge there are bars.

"If you repeat your mantra regularly, all your problems with solve them selves." *Swami Satchidananda*

"Bungalow Billy," he was so silly, so willy-nilly, don't you agree, he was such a killer-dilly?

Peace and love are inseparable twins.

We don't have to make love, we already have it, and we should try to remember that when we make love.

Where do flowers come from? Bobby, a wide eyed, 4 year old little boy, asked me. I said they come from a tree. Then he said where does the tree come from? I said from the ground. Then he said, where does the ground come from? I said the ground comes from the Earth. Then he said, where does the Earth come? I said someplace in the sky. And then he said, where does the sky come from? And before I could answer, he said, who do you think taught birds to fly, and people to cry? Before I could answer, I wasn't sure what I would say, he fell asleep in my arms, gave me time to think about it, should he ask again on another day.

Every moment of our lives, we have a chance to
<u>choose</u> psychological peace of mind, or love, or
to see the world through some version of conflict.

"Let me respectfully remind you,
Life and death are of supreme importance.
Time swiftly passes by and opportunity is lost.
Each of us should strive to awaken…
Awaken… take heed!
Do not squander your life!"

Zen Mountain Monastery

Disadvantages Of Meditation

Understanding the meaning of love is a progressive realization of inter-dependent origination.

Organic is more than a table set, it's a mind set.
Ego mind invented competition.

"The only way of knowing a person is to love them without hope." *Walter Benjamin*

You can't save someone who's drowning if they think they're swimming.

Choose peace, become peace.

Thinking with ego mind is like playing ping-pong with yourself.

Attempting to solve outer world problems before solving inner world problems is like a dog chasing its tail. What would it do if it caught it?

"We are forlorn like children, experienced like old men, we are crude and sorrowful and superficial—I believe we are lost." *Erich Maria Remarque, All Quiet on the Western Front*

The right method for the wrong person, is the wrong method.

"There is no reason to constantly attempt to figure everything out." *Michael A. Singer*

Narcissism is another word for unconscious fear. It's saying: I can't trust anyone to love me, so I'll just love myself. No one can do it better.

I've become more patient lately, I've found things come faster that way.

Those we meet in our dreams, who are they? Why do they come when they do? What is the meaning of what they say?

The ego mask hides a spiritual pandemic.

Music speaks with certainty what words hint at.

Meditation is thought. Whatever you're thinking about you're meditating on.

The ego mind created the physical world. How was the ego mind created?

The karmic mind is a stressful thought system.

Some people can predict the future because it's already happened.

The only thing to be convinced of regarding your karmic unconscious mind is that it's unconscious. And that . . . it is directing your behavior.

Hello Stranger

Alone with the mirror in secret he met,
to discuss his life's forget,
to see things he might regret.

I'm afraid to be alone with you
for reasons I can't explain said he.
After all our time together
I'm not sure I know who you are.
Are you me?

I can fool others but I can't fool you.
I stare at you and questions arise that
I've never thought of before,
questions I have no answers for.

But I mustn't let anyone see me this way,
I have a closet full of disguises to wear
when I go back out the door, when I go back to being
who I've never been before.

A declaration of ego-karmic independence is the great need of this world's inhabitants. Including the writer.

After all is said and done cause-and-effect are one.

Ego mind is a lawyers dodge.

All physical thoughts first originate in ego/karma mind, including genetics. Without ego mind there would no genetics.

For different reasons neither peace nor ego negotiate.

"What if God was one of us? Just a slob like one of us? Just a stranger on the bus trying to make his way home?" *Joan Osborne, "One Of Us"*

The ego mind keeps running in place wondering when it will arrive at its destination.

Karma's God is the ego, And it fears its own vengeance, should it disobey.

"We are what we feel and perceive. If we are angry, we are the anger." *Thich Nhat Hanh*

"We cannot swim for new horizons until you have courage to lose sight of the shore." *William Faulkner*

Ego mind is a spiritual/psychological coma.

"It's better to lose your ego to the one you love, than to lose the one you love to your ego." *John Keats*

When the student is ready the ego appears.

"You know me as you see me, not as I actually am." *Immanuel Kant*

"You have to grow from the inside out. None can teach you; none can make you spiritual. There is no other teacher but your own soul." *Swami Vivekananda*

"I was educated once — it took me years to get over it." *Mark Twain*

"You have your way. I have my way. As for the right way, the correct way, and the only way, it does not exist." *Friedrich Nietzsche*

You can't tame the tiger. You can, however leave the jungle.

It's possible to be someone we don't want to be, to live a life we don't want to live, to live it for so long, that we forget we're living it.

There's only one thing to remember, there's only one thing to forget

The ego invented karma to prove it was real.

Only those who feel they are losers have the insatiable need to win.

Difficulty sleeping is incorrectly named; it should be called: ego-somnia.

Stress is like a car still going down the street while parked.

If too many people become upscale, the ego mind will invent upper-upscale!

Marriage is an ego/karmic idea. How can what was never separated believe it must be joined?

I found an umbrella in my pillowcase. It's hard to sleep in the rain, but sometimes you have to because the weather is so unpredictable.

Only in growing old can we fully experience what it feels like being young, as well as the so-called benefits accrued to both.

Time passes slowly when one is in a hurry.

Fear is the unconscious mind aware of, and watching itself.

"Die the death of the ego and be reborn spiritually even in this very life." *Swami Prahavananda*

Ego mind never forgets it has nothing to remember.

Good news to the karmic ego mind is something like going to the oral surgeon, and being told you don't need a root canal; but you do need to have your gums removed.

The ego is a painful thought.

Everyone who has an ego should receive an Academy Award for acting like someone they're not, for directing the show, for scripting the plot.

"If you want to be creative, stay in part a child, with the creativity and invention that characterizes children before they are deformed by adult society." *Jean Piaget*

If ego-karma wrote the book it would've been called, "Alice In Thunderland."

Karma is love at past sight.

Time waits for no one, which doesn't give us much wiggle room.

Listening with ego is like insisting on wearing a hearing aid with no batteries.

The material world was not made to work.

Ego minds ability to care for us is comparable to getting a root canal from a foot doctor.

"Ego mind is invisible to those who can't see it."
Meryl S., New York

Ego mind created genetics as a distraction.

Ego mind is its own best friend. Ego mind has no friends.

"Peace is present here and now, in our selves, and in everything we do and see. The question is whether or not we are in touch with it." *Thich Nhat Hanh*

"At times of giant steps in the soul's evolutionary expansion there are moments of great insecurity."
Emmanuel's Book - Book One

Not knowing we're lost,
it's a drag, its inhumane, it's like Ukraine.
Windshield wipers stopped working long ago,
still can't stop singing that Creedence song.
"Who'll Stop The Rain"

All the hallowed, and not so hallowed, educational systems of the world have still have not taught humans how to prevent war. Is there something wrong here?

If time doesn't exist, numbers men are useless; they don't add up.

"One man practicing kindness in the wilderness is worth all the temples this world pulls." *Jack Kerouac, The Dharma Bums*

We become what we fight with.

Who is to blame; consumers up to their necks in debt; or the noose makers bayonet?

The ego loves to read between the lines because there's nothing there.

The ego causes its own insurrection.

The ego world is a construction zone, always in need of repair.

Karma is the waiting room of the world.

Ego always arrives on time for an appointment never made.

Ego's only goal is to deny the experience, the emptiness of its perceived loss.

The ego invented "King" so it could worship at its own throne.

The official next half of ego/karma life begins when puberty personality encounters every day reality. If not resolved, adolescent personalities become old age fatalities.

There comes a time when your ceiling meets your floor, when you can't take it anymore. Emboldened with or without income or outcome, you look for the door.

When will we humans grow suspicious of our need to watch horror movies, war movies, movies projecting physical or psychological violence of any kind, like in boxing or football?

Ego is an escape hatch leading back in.

Choose again on this karmic day.

Four handed piano is a good way to play a relationship song. Each player plays a part of the sane song in their own way.

The ego escalator goes up, goes down, goes nowhere, goes round and round.

Ego mind is a juggler that cannot stop juggling. In its karmic way it loves juggling, but is in constant fear of dropping the ball.

"You must have a spirit of prayer, or you will find it hard to persevere. Pray with great faith in God, and God will take care of everything." *Mother Theresa*

"The ego mind is like a bottomless empty plate of lasagna layers that always wants desert no matter how full it is." *Ann Marie L. Bonasera*

Ego knows the ropes no - no - no . . . ego is the ropes.

Ego mind is in constant stress; stress is a pretty word for conflict; conflict is a pretty word for war; war is a pretty word for ego.

"Few things are more rewarding than a child's open uncalculating devotion." *Vera Brittain*

"Mankind's greatest gift, also its greatest curse, is that we have free choice. We can make our choices built from love or from fear." *Elisabeth Kübler-Ross*

When the world has taught us enough we will willing to let go of all the world has taught us

Ego mind invented sin to make us feel guilty.

All kinds of karma are the same. Like any kind of sports game, no matter how many times you win, you must return and try to win again.

Glamour and glitz, high fashion tricks, they knew how to get their kicks. Still, they never saw it coming. Too close to the edge, too tired from running. All this will end when mine is yours, when yours is mine. When there are no more peace treaties left to sign. When there are no more words left to rhyme. When mine is yours, when yours is mine.

Memories missed remain, but nothing you see remains the same. You can't take the past with you, but until you learn that, you will always try and never succeed.

There are two days in the year that we cannot do anything, yesterday and tomorrow. *Mahatma Gandhi*

Karma and Watcher mind thoughts are both cumulative.

The psychological concept of time's purpose is to help us choose to see with Spiritual vision.

"Everything depends on inner change; when this has taken place, then, and only then does the world change." *Martin Buber*

With every thought you have you have a chance to choose to free yourself from your self created karma.

Karma is thought recycling.

Beware Of Listening To This Impostor

"The first man having enclosed a piece of ground, bethought himself of saying: This is mine, and found people simple enough to believe him, was the real founder of civil society. From how many crimes, wars and murders, from how many horrors and misfortunes might not any one have saved mankind, by pulling up the stakes, or filling up the ditch, and crying to his fellows, "Beware of listening to this impostor; you are undone if you once forget that the fruits of the earth belong to us all, and the earth itself to nobody."
Jean-Jacques Rousseau, Died July 2, 1778,

There's a thought we can't figure out, peace of mind. And that's because when we try to, it's gone.

"The only journey is the one within." *Rainer Maria Rilke*

Karma confirms to no calling but its own; the dirge of the material world.

Karma is in the eyes of the beholder.

Karma is a foretold conclusion of a foreboding future.

"You need to spend time crawling alone through shadows to truly appreciate what it is to stand in the sun." *Shaun Hick*

"I will be stronger than my sadness." *Jasmine Warga*

Karma is the only problem we have, but until we realize that, we will try to solve all the other problems.

Everything that causes pain, physical or psychological, is karma to be released, let go of, eliminated.

We are all karmic extensions, and karmic projections, of our own fragmented ego mind inventions.

Living life unaware of ego desert mind is like wearing shoes one size too small, and at last getting used to it, and buying shoes that all fit that way.

If we don't make up our mind, ego mind will make it up for us . . . will make us up.

The ego is a one way street that goes both ways in the same direction.

The major problem of karma is that all people and places must change, while all memories stay the same.

"We must let go of the life we have planned, so as to accept the one that is waiting for us." *Joseph Campbell*

"The only journey is the one within." *Rainer Maria Rilke*

"If the doors of perception were cleansed everything would appear to man as it is, infinite." *William Blake*

"Older men start wars, younger men fight them." *Albert Einstein*

Eckhart Tolle Quotes

"When I occasionally quote the words of Jesus, or the Buddha, from " A Course In Miracles," or from other teachings, I do so, not to compare, but to draw your attention to the fact that an essence there is an always has been only one spiritual teaching, although it comes in many forms."

"So when you listen to a thought, you are aware not only of the thought, but also of yourself as the witness of the thought."

"Why should we be addicted to thinking? Because you are identified with it, which means that you derive your sense of self from the content and activity of your mind."

"The mind cannot know the tree. It can only know facts or information about the tree. My mind cannot know you, only labels, judgments, facts, and opinions about you."

"Don't judge or analyze what you observe." "Be present as the watcher of your mind."

"The most decisive event in your life is when you discover you are not your thoughts or emotions."

-

Course In Miracles Quotes

"A miracle is a correction."

"The course does not aim at teaching the meaning of love, for that is beyond what can be taught. It does aim, however, at removing the blocks to the awareness of love's presence, which is your natural inheritance."

"Simply do this: Be still, and lay aside all thoughts of what you are and what God is; all concepts you have learned about the world; all images you hold about yourself. Empty your mind of everything it thinks is either true or false, or good or bad, of every thought it judges worthy, and all the ideas of which it is ashamed. Hold onto nothing. Do not bring with you one thought the past has taught, nor one belief you ever learned before from anything. Forget this world, forget this course, and come with wholly empty hands unto your God."

"You should look out from the perception of your own holiness to the holiness of others."

"No one could solve all the problems the world appears to hold. They seem to be on so many levels, in such varying forms, and with such varied content, that they confront you with an impossible situation. All this complexity is a desperate attempt not to recognize the problem."

-

"No one should ever forget that one dreams in the first place, and almost to the exclusion of all else, one's self." *Carl Jung*

Spiritual remembrance is everything, no effort is ever forgotten.

The goal of all Eastern spiritual meditation is to be in the present moment. So let's pause a moment in our daily activities, to ask ourselves, the author included, how can we be in the present moment if we bring past karma along for the ride. Shall you try it now?

This book, or any other books written, about how to undo karma, could not have been written without karma's presence. That is karma's only use.

Karma is a desert where we think we live.

Mantra is a feather duster for karmic mind.

I didn't make my bed this morning and didn't feel guilty. I must be making spiritual progress!

No one has ever taken a breath when it isn't now.

Karma is felicity forgotten.

Karma is absence of love. Absence of love is fear. Fear is belief in the separation. Fear is ego-karma.

As a result of cause and effect, karma is going backwards and forwards at the same time. This means everything that has ever happened, has already happened.

Until we learn to be alone with ourselves we shall always be alone.

We can't control ego mind by trying to control ego mind.

Karma is everything you remember that never happened, happening at once.

War is an ego mind sub-personality.

Karma says you can't take it with you. Spiritual mind says: why would you want to?

"The spiritual journey is one of continuous learning and purification. When you know this, you become humble." *Sogyal Rinpoche*

Whatever you repress you become. Whatever you accept and then choose to let go of, you also become.

If one lives their life in a stressful way long enough, they will not feel normal, fulfilled, or happy, unless they feel stressful. Stress will become their identity, the only thing that will give their life meaning.

Take the time
to see between the spaces,
the spaces
ego space and time places,
places between us all.

Use your life's time
to undo the karmic spaces paradigm
of ego space and time!
Thank you, Dalai Lama! Thank you David Baum!
Thank you Mr. Albert Einstein!

How smart is a smart watch that keeps track of something that doesn't exist?

This book is about finding out how to find peace of mind, having first discovered that you've lost it.

What is karma? Karma is forgetting you're a spiritual being having a human experience.

Karma is overlooking the fact that you are a non-physical being having a physical experience.

"Just by the very nature of our birth, we are on the spiritual journey." *Thomas Keating*

Karma is what never happened happening again.

We're all karma-tose.

Karma is artificial intelligence creating the physical world in its own image, in its own way, in its own time. It can show no mercy, for to do so would be self-betrayal.

Ego desert mind is an undercover form of self hate.

Karma is continuous psychological conflict. It is an unconscious war of revenge against itself.

Karma, or the unconscious mind, has created a cause and effect unreal physical world of personal and interpersonal conflict so as to avoid seeing itself as the cause of all conflict, to avoid seeing itself as both victim and victimizer.

Stress, disappointment, fear, guilt, lack of love, all appear different, yet are all the same.

"The spiritual journey is individual, highly personal. It can't be organized or regulated. It isn't true that everyone should follow one path. Listen to your own truth." *Ram Dass*

Trying to outwit ego mind is like trying to bend your head.

Without the 60s hair, 60s clothes, flower power, the Beatles, we hippies would all look just like regular every day people.

"A lot of parents will do anything for their kids except let them be themselves." *Banksy*

"The most important thing that parents can teach their children is how to get along without them." *Frank A. Clark*

Gradually, we learn not to mistake the bumps in the road for the road.

"The danger of motherhood. you relive your early self, through the eyes of your mother." *Joyce Carol Oates*

"To have peace, teach peace to learn it." *A Course In Miracles*

"What it's like to be a parent: It's one of the hardest things you'll ever do but in exchange it teaches you the meaning of unconditional love." *Nicholas Sparks*

"History, Stephen said, is a nightmare from which I am trying to awake." *James Joyce, Ulysses*

"Forgiveness is the only way to reverse the irreversible flow of history." *Hannah Arendt*

All stress is repressed karmic fear. We should all stop kidding ourselves at the end of the day by saying, 'we had a really stressful day,' and instead accept we had a really fearful day, and then, do something about it.

Old karmic habits are hard to break, especially the ones we don't know we have.

Love of money is an old story, always between strangers.

The ego mind and its manifestations, meaning the person we think we are, is always unconscious.

Tomorrow is a continuous consequence of yesterday in the unwatched karmic mind, seasons come, seasons go, weather is the only constant. Dress accordingly.

"Surround yourself only with people who are going to lift you higher." *Oprah Winfrey*

The ego mind is a work of fiction, created by a work of fiction, for a world of fiction.

I feel so alone when I'm not with my phone, I feel like a head of hair without a comb. I remember once my battery died, and I forgot to bring my charger. I wanted to call my mommy, but I knew she'd disconnected her phone a long time ago. So I drove over, but she wasn't home. She never was when I called. I still have her number, but I'm afraid to try it.

Work at become conscious of projecting another's karma, mistaking it for your own.

The ego desert mind is karma. It cannot help but judge people by the color of their skin, or the color of their hair,, or their education, or social standing, or the way the body looks that they're in.

How can we tell for sure when ego mind has come for us? Anytime we feel a form of stress, doubt, fear, guilt, worry, anger, inability to forgive, all those thought feelings are ego sub-personalities, indicating our inability to forgive others *for what it seems* they have done to us. In short, the perceived absence of *our love,* Spiritual love.

We can't have a dream about something that's never happened before, there isn't anything that hasn't happened before.

Waking up and going to sleep are both different versions of the same thing.

Fear short circuits the minds ability to see clearly.

If love grew on trees, we humans would find a way to trim the branches and cut the leaves, to make it fit our impression of what love should look like.

The next time you're feeling down about your life, your state of karma, watch *"Marie's Story"* on tubi, or wherever you can find it.

"Civilizations should be measured by the degree of diversity attained and the degree of unity retained."
W. H. Auden

Your particular karma was a choice, consciously or unconsciously that you made and are making even as you read this, and determine what meaning you give it. This also goes for reading this book.

"Be thine own palace, or the world's thy jail."
John Donne

Artificial intelligence is by its own definition . . . artificial. So although it will solve many of the world's seeming problems, it will do so artificially, thus creating more of the same.

My hearts an open book, but I had to tear some of the pages out because I just couldn't read them anymore.

Karma gets up every morning convincing itself it has slept.

Welcome to the karmic desert mind, birthplace of the unwatched psychological art form, Depressionism,

Karmic mind is a cause-and-effect domain. And leaving karmic past behind is not an easy choice, but we really have no choice, because it's already gone.

"I lost my smile, I can't remember where I put it. I'll ask the bartender maybe he knows." *Anonymous*

Psychological helpers, come in many forms. Some may appear to cause us anger and despair, but they can help us to see that psychologically speaking, there are no victims or victimizers, we give all we see all the meaning it has.

"The secret of happiness, you see, is not found in seeking more, but in developing the capacity to enjoy less." *Socrates*

If we become used to music playing all the time, silence becomes distracting. If we become used to silence all the time music becomes distracting.

"Knowing how to be solitary is central to the art of loving. When we can be alone, we can be with others without using them as a means of escape." *Bell Hooks*

At some point it may occur to ask ourselves: Why have we made up this karma world?

"I found I had less and less to say, until finally, I became silent, and began to listen. I discovered in the silence, the voice of God." *Soren Kierkegaard*

"The true meaning of love one's neighbor is not that it is a command from God which we are to fulfill, but that through it and in it we meet God." *Martin Buber*

Given karmic unconscious is an ego extension of our individual unconscious mind, we are all, to some extent, at all times, unconscious.

Creating the meaningless with the meaningless is karma's idea of meaning.

To study neurology separate from psychology is like to trying to eat with your mouth closed.

"We are neurotic when we are not what God meant us to be." *Marie-Louise von Franz.*

"The camera introduces us to unconscious optics as does psychoanalysis to unconscious impulses."
Walter Benjamin

The only way out of here is remembering you've never been here.

"Spiritual practice is not what you are doing, it is what you are thinking. It is with the mind we do everything. All of your problems would solve themselves if you were regular in your meditation." *Swami Satchidananda*

"Wherever we go, we bring our mind with us, so the world we see is subjective, our own predisposition conditions our impression of all events." *Carl Jung*

"History, despite its wrenching pain, cannot be unlived, but if faced with courage, need not be lived again." *Maya Angelou*

"May you always know the truth
And see the light surrounding you"
Bob Dylan, "Forever Young"

Ego mind talks to itself, teaching itself what it already knows, making believe it's something new.

Think about what your life would be like, had you been walking backward all the time, but thought you were walking forward. That's what ego-karma mind has us doing.

Ego karmic mind first creates and then gives names to all the psychological and physical diseases it creates, and then begins trying to finding solutions for them.

"We had thought that we were human beings making a spiritual journey; it may be truer to say that we are spiritual beings making a human journey."
Pierre Teilhard de Chardin

"It may be that when we no longer know what to do, we have come to our real work, and that when we no longer know which way to go, we have begun our real journey." *Wendell Berry*

Ego mind is a self created humankind double bind. On one hand it needs competition to exist. On the other hand it MUST win or face the fist.

We make up a story about someone in our mind, and when they don't live up to it, we blame them.

Hurricanes, tornadoes, earthquakes, tsunamis, things like that, they don't ask permission to come, they just come. Ego mind is like that; just blowin' in the wind.

"It's being here now that's important. There's no past and there's no future. Time is a very misleading thing. All there is ever, is the now. We can gain experience from the past, but we can't relive it; and we can hope for the future, but we don't know if there is one."
George Harrison

"The ultimate lesson all of us have to learn is that unconditional love, includes not only others but ourselves as well." *Elisabeth Kubler-Ross*

"Mindfulness is the art of experiencing the nonexistence of the past and the future."
Mokokoma Mokhonoana

"The measure of society is how it treats the weakest members." *Thomas Jefferson,*

My heart is an open book, please read with love and compassion, I will attempt the same with your book.

Your karma expressed when the light turns red, as you try to beat the yellow through the intersection.

"The geographical pilgrimage is the symbolic acting out of an inner journey. The inner journey is the interpolation of the meanings and signs of the outer pilgrimage. One can have one without the other. It is best to have both." *Thomas Merton*

"Go outside. Don't tell anyone, and don't bring your phone. Start walking and keep walking until you no longer know the road like the palm of your hand, because we walk the same roads day in and day out, to the bus and back home and we cease to see. We walk in our sleep, and we teach our muscles to work without thinking, and I dare you to walk where you have not yet walked, and I dare you to notice. Don't try to get anything out of it, because you won't. Don't try to make use of it, because you can't. And that's the point. Just walk, see, sit down if you like. And be. Just be, whatever you are, with whatever you have, and realize that that is enough to be happy." *Charlotte Eriksson*

Choose compassion, and become what you choose.

Ego-karma resembles flashing red tail lights that are nearly impossible to see until we are right up on them, in a raging rain storm, often too late to stop.

Ego-karma has a purpose: to be seen and let go;

Ego mind only sees through the past. And in that seeing, creates its future . . . like a rolling stone.

"We are all just prisoners here of our own device."
The Eagles, "Hotel California"

The brain does not feel or love, it responds only to the requests of the mind.

Due to cause-and-effect, karma has become every thought you will ever have, unless you can find a way to realize you are the Watcher and choose differently.

Karma is conflict, karma is also called ego.

We choose every moment of our lives, and so we have a chance to choose psychological peace of mind or love, to see the world through some version of conflict, or peace.

If you came to believe nothing ever happened,
would you try to figure out how?
If you came to believe nothing ever happened
would you try to solve all the problems
that nothing ever happened too?
And if you did, how would you go about it?
And how would you know when you were through?

When someone pushes your ego button, thank them for helping you find your karma.

Understanding love is a progressive realization of dependent origination.

"Through violence you may solve one problem, but you sew the seeds for another." *Dalai Lama*

Nothing we see or experience, no matter the people, or circumstances, has any meaning except what we give it. There are only two types of meanings we can give so called others, and at the same time, ourselves. The first is seeing through our habituated, historical past, the ego-karma-mind. The second is free of the past, the Watcher-Chooser-Spiritual-Mind.

The historically programmed ego mind is pushed to the wall to control what it's afraid of. And it is afraid of everything, including itself. So then, what does it do when it gets to the wall?

A habit is a sub-personality to which we have given autonomy.

We're straphangers on history's ego seesaw.

I've become more patient lately. I've found things come faster that way.

We can run from ourselves,
we can run from others,
we can even run from God.
But run we cannot,
from the consequences of our choices.

Ego mind never forgets it has nothing to remember.

"At times of giant steps in the soul's evolutionary expansion there are moments of great insecurity."
Emmanuel's Book - Book One

Ego mind created genetics as a distraction.

Ego mind is its own best friend. Ego mind has no friends.

"This whole creation is essentially subjective, and the dream is the theater where the dreamer is at once: scene, actor, prompter, stage manager, author, audience, and critic." *Carl Jung*

"The spiritual journey is one of continuous learning and purification. When you know this, you become humble." *Sogyal Rinpoche*

"Just by the very nature of our birth, we are on the spiritual journey." *Thomas Keating*

Karma is what never happened happening again.

Karma is continuous psychological conflict. It is an unconscious war of unknowing revenge against itself.

Every entrance has an exit, except one.

Ego desert mind is an undercover form of self hate.

"Be present as the watcher of your mind." *Eckhart Tolle*

Karma is the result of past actions in the material world.

Eastern, spiritual psychology's teach there is no material world.

The only purpose of karmic mind is for us to become aware of it, and find a way to release from it.

Your particular karma was, is, a choice, consciously or unconsciously you made and are making even as you read this and determine what meaning you give it.

The past and the future have already happened, the only thing we can do about that is to release ourselves, that is to find a way to psychologically release ourselves from its artificial psychological conditions.

The only way to release the future is to release the past.

If we cannot, forgive, and forgiving has nothing to do with the other person, we ourselves carry the pain, the disappointment, the anger and hurt of our inability to forgive within us, and in that way harm only ourselves. The benefit of forgiveness is self experienced and has nothing to do with anyone but ourselves.

Karma is a sold out concert with nobody there.

I played catching up so long I forgot I was caught up in catching up.

Lack of forgiveness permeates and influences every thought we have about everyone, whether it seems we love them or not, and everything we think, do or feel, because we give everything we see all the meaning it has for us.

Fear is only as strong as your avoidance of it. The greater your reluctance to see the fear, to accept it, to embrace it with love, the more power you allow it.

"I am certain that nobody can always be responsible for what other people are." "You can only be responsible for who you are." *Paul Newman*

"Be willing to be a beginner every single morning." *Meister Eckhart*

First we make our habits, then our habits make us — or break us.

"Never look back unless
you're planning to go that way."
Henry David Thoreau

Ego mind needs money for validation. Money is neutral. The only question to ask ourselves about money, or anything else is: What is it for?

"It's time for you to move, realizing that the thing you are seeking is also seeking you." *Iyanla Vanzant*

Slow and steady wins the race, when we begin to realizes there is no race.

Where ego is involved no human problem will ever be solved.

During some unplanned moments alone at home, you never know who you might run into.

Only ego mind can be famous.

Our relationship with our self determines our relationship with so called others, IS our relationship with ourselves.

Choose now, there is no other time here.

"You know, my Mom and Dad, well they're really nice people, I mean I love 'em, they take good care of our dogs and cats, even buy them organic food to eat, pet 'em, let 'em sleep in the bed with them! But then, they go out and eat dead cow and chicken sandwiches? It all seems very weird to me, but look, I'm just a little boy, maybe when I grow up, I'll understand it better." *Little boy who lives near me.*

Why Did Ego-Karma Mind Invent Football?

Ego-karma needs an enemy and a conquerer, a winner and a loser in all things, to validate its existence. It does not care who suffers in its gladiator, neanderthal, game. Football fits its needs perfectly, because no football team finally loses, or finally wins, but must both win and lose over and over, again and again.

In this way football plays out our personal and collective, historical, educated, acculturated, unconscious ego-karma needs to be both a winner and a loser - you can't be one without the other - in this way stay in constant state of uncertainty and conflict.

Why do adults encourage young people to play a game where they have to wear helmets to prevent brain injury in their effort?

- "NFL's Nick Buoniconti, Jim Kiick and Jake Scott, 1972 Miami Dolphins, were found to have C.T.E., the brain disease linked to head hits, bringing to six the number of players from that team." *New York Times, 2/13/22.*

- "At least four fixtures of Alabama's great teams of the 1960s had chronic traumatic encephalopathy, or C.T.E., at their deaths." *New York Times, 8/7/2022.*

"Meiko Locksley was found to have had a degenerative brain disease (C.T.E) often associated with football. His father, the head coach at Maryland, is still reckoning with the implications. C.T.E. can only be diagnosed, with certainty, posthumously."
Locksley said, "I always thought, like, how do you go from a normal 21-year-old Division I football-playing person to, literally six months later, saying you hear people in the basement of an apartment where you lived on the eighth floor and you don't have a basement?"

The brain of Meiko Locksley is one of 152 belonging to contact-sport athletes under the age of 30 that were donated between 2008 and 2022 to the UNITE Brain Bank and studied by researchers at Boston University. In a paper published Monday (8/28/23) in JAMA Neurology, the researchers reported that 63 of the athletes, or 41.4 percent of them, had C.T.E. Most were football players who never played past college, sometimes not past high school. One was 17." *New York Times, August, 2023*

- The NFL will pay $765 million to settle a lawsuit brought by more than 4,000 retirees with advanced dementia and other issues from long-term effects of head trauma. Adopted: *New York Times, August, 2013*

- Tyler Lewellen, a junior defensive back, Arlington High School,Riverside, California, died from severe head trauma five days after collapsing on the sidelines during a scrimmage. Tyler was one of more than a dozen high school players who died this year as a direct result of playing football. Adopted: *New YorkTimes, December, 2013*

"It is no longer debatable," said Dr. Ann McKee, a neuropathologist, who examined 202 deceased football players.

A broad survey of her findings was published in The Journal of the American Medical Association. Of the 202 players, 111 of them played in the N.F.L. — and 110 of them had chronic traumatic encephalopathy, or C.T.E., a degenerative disease believed to be caused by repeated blows to the head. Adopted: *New York Times, July, 2017*

- Bubba Smith, the NFL star and actor, who passed in 2011, is the 90th former NFL player to have had the degenerative brain disease, CTE The disease has been linked to NFL repeated head trauma. Adopted: *New York Times, May, 2016.*

They started Playing Football as Kids, and Died Before 30 With C.T.E. Researchers found that the players had C.T.E., the brain disease linked to hits to the head. If their families could go back, would they still let them play? *New York Times, November 17, 2023*

A new study by the Laureate Institute for Brain Research, University of Tulsa, Tulsa, Oklahoma, shows brains of college football players are different then other students, adding concern that sports-related hits to the head may have lingering effects even in athletes who have never had a concussion. *Adopted: New York Times, May, 2014.*

As a collective society, why do we do this? Is this how we "love our brain injured neighbor as our self?" What are the psychological needs of both grown adult men, and women, that cause them to enjoy watching young boys compete with each other in such a brutal way? Who is it they are really watching?

Why do we pay money, eat hot dogs. eat pizza, drink beer, have fun, cheer and watch? Why do you think we use young girls to cheer the football boys on?

Head on.

The Nuclear Football

Why have we named it the "nuclear football," or the atomic football, or even a football? "It is a briefcase, the contents of which are to be used by the president of the United States to communicate and authorize a nuclear attack while away from fixed command centers, such as the White House Situation Room, or the Presidential Emergency Operation Center." *Wikipedia*

"Breathe. Let go. And remind yourself that this very moment is the only one you know you have for sure." *Oprah Winfrey*

I knew a woman who had no father to love her. Her conscious understanding of his loving face didn't exist. Karmically she met a man she loved. And he loved her, but ego mind perceived him as her father! It blinded her to what she now had, what she was looking for: A loving man, unlike her dad. She loved him dearly, but was afraid to know it. Gradually he grew afraid to show it. Ego mind insured they'd never outgrow it.

You can't negotiate with ego mind.

History is a treadmill always going in the same direction.

"It's almost always people whose lamented busyness is purely self imposed. They're busy because of their own ambition or drive or anxiety, because they're addicted to busyness and dread what they might have to face in its absence." *Anxiety: The Busy Trap, New York Times, July 2012*

It was a dreary day, no sun, heavy rain, loud thunder. I couldn't go outside, so I stayed inside, used my umbrella.

"History is a vast early warning system."
Norman Cousins

Sunny mirrored playground — quacking ducks floating 'round — until suddenly by humans found. Suddenly, harsh banging loud repeating sounds — bullets pounding rounds. Then, cheering humans catch in hand, homebound, leaving quacking ducks playground. *Dedicated to Bungalow Bill*

We can't fall in or out of love, but we can think we can.

History is the ego minds method of maintaining control.

Me: I'm just sage-ing, warmly welcoming old aging. Like that old timer in that French movie "Avenue Montaigne." He was explaining, while champagne-ing. "There comes a time - when time passing - becomes time remaining."

The only difference between men and women is they are the same in different ways.

Why do some people have Ralph Lipchitz's ego logo on their clothing?

Inflation is a word for milking the cow dry.

The egos version of YouTube is MeTube.

Choose again to see with Spiritual Vision.

Only human beings give our offspring up for adoption, circumstances may dictate this as a preferable option. Why have we chosen those types of circumstances?

San Juan de la Cruz should have phrased it "dark night of the ego." The soul doesn't have a dark night.

Dreams appear in a predetermined rehash. Ego karmic mind dishes up what was ordered in the past.

I do not know who you are, or when you will read this. I do know cause and effect are simultaneous, so you are reading this now, when you are supposed to.

"Being deeply loved by someone gives you strength, while loving someone deeply gives you courage."
Lao Tzu

Ego mind creates wars to blame others for wars creation.

Karma is similar to an all natural muffin made with artificial ingredients.

Ego mind creates governments, that create weapons, to save us from governments, that create weapons.

We can't hide from others, only from ourselves.

As I grow old,
I want to grow old with you,
and all things you help see me through.

As I grow old,
now and then,
morning sun rises again,
and so do I again with you

I look at shared skies of blue with you,
my very first, my very last,
my always there rendezvous.

There's nothing more, nothing less,
nothing else left to do,
I want to grow old with you.

The only way someone can sell you out is if you're for sale.

Somethings must be done alone, but not necessarily on one's own.

There will not be complete free individual existence until there is free collective existence.

Ego mind creates enemies to ride shot gun in defense of its innocence.

There is no such thing as a small decision.

"Love, Serve, Remember. Be Here Now." *Ram Dass*

The karmic world's
most consequential climate changing conformation
isn't prevention of weather devastation.
It's for a growing global awareness
of inter-dependent origination.

The ego mind is like a business you start that then runs itself, with or without you, whether you like it or not.

The ego mind invented loneliness and as a favor, all its correctives.

Each breath is a new beginning, a letting go. But must be consciously chosen to be so.

Love can be right in front of your face, but when you can't see it; it's not there.

Before you lay all your cards on the table; first know who you're playing with; second, at first, place them face down.

The ego mind is a jigsaw puzzle with a missing piece. It knows it will never be complete. It is terrified of that awareness.

Your ego mind doesn't care about you.

History is a mind blip, over the moment it began.

Ego mind always looks outside itself for what it thinks it doesn't have.

"Oxfam, an international group of charitable organizations focused on alleviating global poverty reported the world's 85 richest people have the same wealth as the poorest 50%, that is to say, 3.5 billion people. Also that the 80 richest people have the same wealth as the poorest 50%." BBC news, January, 19, 2015

Let's believe in the time of no history left to defend.

God bless us never lose
what we have right now:
Freedom from the fire.

God bless us never lose
what we have right now;
warm cup of tea together made,
laughter side by side,
hands held
across the table
on the ride:
Freedom from the fire.

God bless all never lose what we have right now;
loving determination to consciously choose:
Freedom from the fire.

Youth is a passing fad.

History is all green lights in the wrong direction. That's why it repeats itself.

If you think the paranoids are after you, they will be.

Anti-aging is a deep state unconscious ego mind plot.

If God is not unconscious there can be no unconscious.

Questions do not matter. To ask Original Mind for the answer is the answer.

When observing the unconscious in dreams it is crucial to our state of well-being, that we remain aware it is unconscious, therefore in an unalterable state of paranoia. It does not care about you. It does not care about itself.

Neediness is an exclusive ego personality property.

We live in a space suit, ego has named it: body.

Nothing worth holding on to is worth holding onto too tightly.

For one-to-one relationships to work we should work with them like we do our iPhone. If we tap too hard or soft, they resist working.

The ego needs open mind surgery

Self-reliance relies on peace of mind.

Original minds web address is: peace.calm

Original Spiritual Mind helps place us where we can see our suffering, have compassion for others who suffer, and see there are no others.

No longer will I live like an ambulance perpetually trapped in time, racing down the same old streets, lights flashing, sirens blazing: A patient, impatient to find!

What is this thing called the ego?
Where did it come from?
Who made it?
How does it live? Why does it live? Does it live?

Are all egos different?
Does the ego ever sleep?
Does the ego ever wake up?
How do we know when we have met the ego?
What do we say when we do?

There is no such thing as luck of the draw, we draw what we seesaw. Cause and effect, that's ego law.

Check out "Ego Watchers Diet;" it's free at the Spiritual Mind closest to you.

"When the word Yoga is mentioned most people immediately think of some physical postures for relaxing and limbering up the body. This is one aspect of the Yogic science, but actually only a very small part and relatively recent in development. The physical Yoga, Hatha Yoga, was primarily designed to facilitate the real practice of Yoga, name the understanding and complete mastery over the mind. So the actual meeting of Yoga is science of the mind." *Swami Satchidananda*

Ego experiences are always déjà vu, everything comes into view as new.

Meditation: It's like a piano tuner for the mind.

Beneath each burst of jealousy is a heart asking for love.

Memories fit like a glove and after a while we forget we have them on.

Some nations believe in the rule of law. Some nations believe in the law of rule.

Memories are history's henchmen.

Ego cards are all the same, only the players change.

Revolutions can sometimes be made without outer armies, but never without inner battles.

"You say you want a revolution? You better free your mind instead." *Beatles, "Revolution"*

Forest Gump

"What's the matter mama?

Mama: I'm dying Forest.

Forest: Why are you dying mama?

Mama: My time, it's just my time. Don't you be afraid sweetheart, death is just a part of life, something we're all destined to do. I didn't know but I was destined to be your mama. I did the best I could.

Forest: You did good mama.

Mama: Well, I happen to believe you make your own destiny, you have to do the best with what God gave you.

Forest: What's my destiny mama?

Mama: You're going to have to figure that out for yourself. Life is a box of chocolates Forest, you never know what you're going to get." *From the movie "Forest Gump"*

The ego invented science so it could explain the unexplainable to itself over and over, and over, etc.

Empty lives can seem to be full of empty things to do.

We die while living. If we deny that, we do not live.

When humankind has achieved herd immunity from the ego mind pandemic, governments will gradually punch the clock.

When I was a boy in Brooklyn I was so busy being happy I didn't know I was happy. Then I grew up.

"If men could learn from history, what lessons it might teach us. But passion and party blind our eyes, and the light which experience gives us is a lantern on the stern, which shines only on the waves behind us."
Samuel Taylor Coleridge

Renoir and Monet, they helped evolve the way people saw things in their ways. The Beatles, Dylan, flower power, evolved those same things in their chosen days.

I dare you come attack me said the ego turtle to the lion! For if you do you will see you made a big mistake, when all your teeth begin to break.
(Sometimes it's good to go into our shell as long as we remember to come out when all is well.)

Angelica's Kitchen - Myron and Lily

Back in the 1990's there was a restaurant in New York I used to go to just about every night, "Angelica's Kitchen." A nice woman named Leslie owned it, it was on 12th off Second, heading towards First. The actress, Kerry Washington, she wasn't famous yet, worked there as a hostess. I remember one night I came in and she was all excited about getting a part in a Pepsi commercial or something like that. They had a great manager, Dennis, he knew everybody by name.

They had a Community table there, and there were a bunch of us that used to go there all the time, this went on for several years, probably six or seven, and we all got to know each other, and we'd look forward to seeing and talking with each other each night. The restaurant is gone now, the people leasing it to Leslie, made the rent too high, and the restaurant become impossible to maintain even after raising prices, which Leslie was not happy about doing.

There was a great married couple who would go there, both of them were very aware of everyday going's on in the world, which we would all talk about, Myron and Lily. Myron was 86, Lily was 83. They both were former teachers in the New York City school system. Myron liked to go shopping before coming to the community table, he'd always come go the table carrying something, always to Lily's concerned look.

Her words to him, and the look on her face when she would talk to him, was because she was concerned about his health, and told him he shouldn't do that, but he did it anyway. We never knew what specific health issue Myron had. Myron was a very happy man, always had a funny story, or a joke to tell.

Well, we didn't see them for a week or two, and we all thought, or felt, that Myron had died, which turned out to be true. After Myron died, I used to walk Lily up First Avenue, to Fourteenth. She would always stop and shop for vegetables or fruit at a place on First, and then we'd walk to the 14th St. bus stop at First, where she'd wait for the bus, then we'd hug and say goodbye.

Well, we didn't see Lily for a week or so, I'm not sure now why I didn't think of getting her phone number or address, checking on her, but anyway, when she came back to the Community table, she told us that Myron had died. About three or four weeks after Myron's passing, Lily told us all about two dreams that she had had, where Myron told her he was fine, and not to worry. Then one night, she told us she had a third dream. In this one Myron told her he was moving onto another level, but not to worry, everything was OK, but he wouldn't be able to talk with her anymore. 🙏

We are afraid of solitude, of silence, more than anything else, afraid of what we might see in ourselves.

If we grow up too fast, we will always want to revisit, re-live the past, to claim the bypassed.

Winning and losing are the same to the ego mind.

Ego invented words, lot's of words, made up lot's and lot's of languages, all different, to make it harder for us to communicate with each other, to make us think we are all different.

There's only one choice we can make that has no drawbacks: Mantra.

Accommodate the unconscious, hear what it has to say, or it will have its way.

A West Village psychic told me Chuck Berry was a famous piano player around the 17th or 18th century! She said when he came back this time, lot's of things had changed, but he still loved music, and that this time he played a guitar, and sang, and gave us clues: "Roll over Beethoven, dig these rhythm and blues."

We think we write, but we can only scribe from either or one or two sources.

Ego invented archaeology, so it could study itself.

The desperation of loneliness makes the wind blow either way. We fight against what we need most.

Knowing to exit a burning building is more important than knowing how the fire began.

Songs are short versions of long books put to music.

We should embrace spiritual mind practices of our choosing, if not for ourselves, but for those being born, for those yet to come.

Gradually, as we give up our desire for the expected, the unexpected appears.

When the idea of justice was conceived, at that instant was ego perceived.

"There was a missing person inside of myself and I needed to find him." *Bob Dylan Chronicles"*

"The greatest of faults is to be conscious of none." *Thomas Carlyle*

Ego mind covertly invented wires so it could invent wireless.

"Be more concerned with your character than your reputation, because your character is what you really are, while your reputation is merely what others think you are." *John Wooden*

Golf is a form of ego concentration that could also be used to practice Spiritual Mind hole in ones.

As we release the past with mantra, we gradually give up our old identity. It is "within the process itself" that *consciously* we begin to recall we are spiritual beings having a human experience.

I have no credentials no pedigree. I have no masters, no PhD, no BBC. Even the process of learning to read and write, though very valuable, helped convince me I am no longer free.

The most important exercise begins in the mind.

It's easier to show who you are, than to know who you are.

Millions of year from now, think of it dear reader, anthropologist ego diggers, digging into historical records of our times, those they can find: investigating, evaluating, decaffeinating; our militarism, materialism, sexism, boxing matches, our acculturated adolescence; our billionaire city steeples, those diggers will see us then, as we now see the cave peoples.

The ego mind is a gated community.

History is the ego minds method of maintaining control.

In moments of despair we are given opportunity to awaken. But the choice must be consciously taken.

Pray like there's no tomorrow, there isn't.

I used to worry all the time. Now, I hardly worry. And you know what; I'm worried about that!

Nothing but your own ego mind can deceive you.

When the mind dreams the thoughts most needed to be seen make the scene.

The way ego mind works is something like your right foot falls asleep and you're not aware of it until you try to stand up.

Time is a cause and effect invention of man, used to keep track of time since time never began.

History's darkness should awaken necessity for light. But history teaches only its own.

Until humans learn to inner govern, governments will be seen necessary to keep us free. As long as we let ego mind keep us hanging on, dead on, the world will not be free of its self created, unconscious hoax; its "you versus me" jokes.

The world is your personal movie screen, your mind your personal projector. What shall you watch today? Chose anew.

Leaving the past behind can be very difficult even though it's gone every second.

Laws can be interpreted differently. Love cannot.

Others can make your day, but it's good to consider doing it yourself in case they don't.

Reincarnation is an interesting idea. I'll have to think about it next time.

We shouldn't go looking for trouble, if we need some it will find us, and then we can choose what to do.

With meditation nothing changes except how we perceive things. And with that all things change.

There are only two states of mind, dystopia and utopia.

The ego mind sees through the past, thereupon creating the future.

Efforts and results always meet. They don't always shake hands.

The best of things can't be planned.

If you don't move on with your life, your life will move on without you.

The old bulb wears out, so you get a new one. That's reincarnation.

In the course of your life if it turns out that mantra is a path for you, and you take the time to understand it, to learn what it is, what it says, what it does, you will find, though not overnight, mantra will solve all the problems you knew you had. And those you didn't know you had.

The Beatles, Bob Dylan, Flower Power, Dr. King, meditation, the Sixties; they were the closest things to sanity we could understand at the time.

I knew someone who was a competitive marathon runner, but couldn't take a quiet walk.

The ego needs stress to assure itself it's real. To assure itself it has enough stress it creates more.

The ego impersonates an empty dinner plate. It always wants more, no matter how much it's had.

We are unconscious pawns, unaware we are terrified of all things, but mostly of waking up.

Once-upon-time I had a dream. It seemed so real it clearly fooled me.

What kind of music would Mozart and Beethoven play if they were around here today? And what about Monet? Wouldn't he be painting Parisians dancing, laughing, rocking all about, to that Isley/Beatles song "Twist and Shout"?

Dreams will wake you, to help you, inspect you, so that you can correct you.

"The only thing we learn from history is that we learn nothing from history. What experience and history teaches us is that people and governments have never learned anything from history, or acted on principles deduced from it." *G.W.F. Hegel*

Ego mind is a dead end Interstate of one way exits.

Ego is the problem causing all problems.

Outer disputes are inner disputes projected outward.

No one gets it right all the time; give us more room for compassion.

Far from the maddening crowd is not far enough.

In ego mind Pinocchio rules.

Al, Martin, And Robert

Al, Martin, And Robert
they're just doin' their job.
They couldn't be doin' it just for the money,
so who is their heartthrob?

Al, Martin, and Robert
how many more violent Bufalino,
"Killers of the Flower Moon,"
blood and guts movies
will you make for us to see?

They paint houses, kill for money,
make Academy Award news,
make Godfather offers we can't refuse.

Why does the world feel
safe as a wick on a candle,
safe as a door without a handle?

Al, Martin, And Robert,
they're just doin' their job,
they couldn't be doin' it for the money,
so who is their ego heartthrob?

"Someone called me; he said, you must be alone.
I said, no, I'm here with my ego."
From, "It's Taken Me a Lifetime to Accept It and Move On,"
Al Pacino on The Godfather: New York Times, March 9, 2022

Ego Mind Makes War Crimes Legal!

Legally defining certain acts of war as
"acceptable war crimes,"
should, but does not yet reveal to enough of us,
the depth, the depravity, the insanity, of our self hate,
stored in the unconscious karmic mind.
Wars will have a realistic chance of ending,
when enough of us each become aware,
of the specific location of wars origination.

"If you hate a person,
you hate something in him
that is part of yourself.
What isn't part of ourselves, doesn't disturb us."
Hermann Hesse

"Never think that war, no matter how necessary,
nor how justified, is not a crime." *Ernest Hemingway*

Eastern spiritual philosophy seeks to comfort us by telling us when we awaken, we will not remember we slept.

If Gandhi, King, Lincoln, Mother Theresa, and those like minded were here today, do you think there'd be anything different in what they'd say?

Everyone who has an ego should receive an Academy Award for acting like someone they're not, for directing the show, for scripting the plot.

We become what we fight with.

We can't forgive others for what they've done, because there are no others.

The colors on a clowns face stand for ego lies, and the colors all began to run as the clown cries.

Music soothes the savage beast, which is good to know should you run into a savage beast willing to listen.

Leo Tolstoy wrote, "Everything that I know…I know only because I love." Let us each dear reader, without denying or confirming Tolstoy's words, each ask ourselves explicitly: What is love?

Ego sleight of hand is difficult to un-big bang.

The ego is a fictional character.

Revenge is a three letter word: ego.

Hatha yoga practices are supplements to mantra
repetition and/or a regular medication practice just as
vitamins are supplements to a diet.

"Technology is advancing, and we are forced to keep
up with it like it or not, so we don't get left behind."
Ishwara Aref, Integral Yoga Institue, San Francisco

The way we think of others is how we think of our
selves. Only to ourselves do we first give each thought.
Illusions take many forms; believe in one - believe in
all.

"If you're going to San Francisco, be sure to wear
some flowers in your hair." *"San Francisco," Scott
McKenzie*

"Land ho" cried the wounded sailors,
make it to shore we must somehow!
Stay the course we must
for which we have charted, if not for us
but for those desert sailors to come, for them,
for genertions after, we must not disavow!
The storm rages - take all hands mates,
hold fast to the bough!"

Would you like to meet your ego mind face to face? It's easy. Try to lose weight, stop smoking, stop drinking, start exercising more, break away from a painful relationship, etc.; try to break any long ingrained habit and find that you can't, and say hello. Anger finds meaning in anger, and over and over with use habituates into an autonomous unconscious sub-personality which believes in itself and its purpose.

Choices are made, results are given, we become what we choose. There are only two choices.

The Awareness is: "Everything there will ever be, everything there is, everything there ever was, since the beginning of beginning-less time." *Author Unknown*

The sun always shines on the other side of the mountain, even on rainy days.

Ego desert mind creates seemingly different versions of our past every moment of our lives, yet all are the same.

We can practice becoming aware that - our need to control or dominate others - differing from directing or inspiring others without intention of outcome, derives and grows out of our own unconscious and thus unaware belief that "it is we" who lack self control.

Ego mind is a virtual reality video game. *Bonnie White*

Understanding we are the watcher of all see, we can realize we are the decision maker, and that we can choose how we perceive the world, ourselves, others. There's a place in the mind that is always watching. We should inquire: What is that place?

In everyday life we often find ourselves in stress provoking circumstances, that never seem to resolve, no matter efforts made. Or if they do resolve, they eventually reappear in other circumstances. Because of their reappearance, we have the opportunity to question ourselves as to "why we continue to repeat these stressful habit patterns," and then doing our *gentle* best, never giving up, find the answer as to why: And there is only one answer, because their is only one problem, and we are watching it.

-

Any event interpreted as our having won or lost, such as winning or losing in sports, in business, in any interaction, must be achieved by means of physical or psychological violence. This is due to cause-and-effect which both automatically, intensifies and increases justification for physical or psychological violence as an ongoing solution for winning, assuring it will be used again and again. The need to win or lose, must first be undone in our mind before winning without winning, and losing without losing can be achieved. Violence, physical or psychological, is never good.

Make the effort to focus your full attention on a single rose, or of a photo or one, or just smell its scent, to experience its beauty, just look at it. Gradually you will not want to understand who planted the rose, where it came from, or how long it will live. *Life's most precious instants cannot be understood, only experienced.* I'm working on it. Will you join me?

The only one way to know something for sure is to experience it.

"Memory is not what the heart desires. That is only a mirror." *J.R.R. Tolkien, The Lord of the Rings*

"Your sacred space is where you can find yourself over and over again." Joseph Campbell

"You can spend all your time making money, you can spend all your love making time." *"Take It To The Limit," Randy Meisner, The Eagles*

The purpose of all teachers, "and we are all teachers," is to listen carefully to questions others may ask us about anything, and without having a prior agenda in mind, suggesting what options there are, but not the "right" way to go.

Ego mind created a one trick pony, karma.

There is no such thing as a meaningless decision. All decisions bring back the past, create the future or accompany freedom from both.

We are the ones responsible for choices, we determine our karma. As Chief Inspector Clouseau would say; "Case sol-ved!"

Every dream we have at night contains all dreams we've ever dreamt.

Ego desert mind means every frantic word it says because it knows it means nothing.

In all things there comes a time to say: we've done our best, we'd best be on our way.

"The Ego is a veil between humans and God." *Rumi*

Anger is a way to justify our inability to forgive ourselves for the inability to forgive ourselves.

Consider that we have lived, and are living many karmic lives simultaneously, each happening once-upon-time, each one thinking it is different.

Next time, you have a dream, like watching a movie, "just watch" your sub personalities and consider that you cannot be what you are watching.

We backstab only ourselves.

The more unconscious a relationship, the more unconscious the results. The participants will not be aware of this believing they are the unconscious.

Ego is undetected cyber warfare in the routers of our minds.

"If you judge people, you have no time to love them."
Mother Teresa

Ego-karma mind is the same as playing chess against yourself, trying to anticipate your next move.

Ego desert mind is a psychological red light masquerading as yellow or green, depending on how many red lights you've run or seen.

If we don't know we are living in a closet, we live in that closet all our lives, not realizing we are in one. Therefore, we never try to open the door to get out. And, we try to get others to come into the closet with us, and play living.

Your author goes along with this quote from Mr. George, as regards this book: "I ask no one who may read this book to accept my views. I ask him to think for himself." *Henry George*

The next time someone says they miss you more than they can say; suggest they give it a try.

No one has ever taken a breath when it isn't now, when it isn't the present moment. This remembering is the benefit of all meditation. If it works for you use it.

Never run after what's running away.

Follow the teachings you feel are right, *not* the teacher.

We will never get enough of what isn't there.

One way we (me as well) can learn what to do when we are battered by life, and consider giving up, is to go online and type in: *"Bridge of Spies/Standing Man."*

Ego mind is so complicated because it contains the past since the past never began.

Karma mind is always recycled.

Ego-karma is a door without a room, so we can't get out or in.

Ego desert mind is psychological quicksand.

Spiritual growth is generally one step forward, two, three, or four more steps back.

While we're asleep at night we're not conscious that we're sleeping. We are Spiritual beings having a physical human experience, it's something like that.

The closest conscious state to leaving the past, the present, and the future behind, is the Awareness.

Have you heard of the cleaning woman of long ago? She'd clean dark dirty places most cleaners wouldn't go. One day when she was done cleaning, that's all I know, she left for a place where all who are finished cleaning go. When we're done cleaning here, we'll meet her there, smile and say, thank you Mother Dear.

Ego-karma desert mind is like a fire engine that has set itself on fire. With its sirens screaming, running red lights, it rushes to put out the fire.

Original mind is your only best friend.

Here is an explanation of meditation and how it works: Whatever you're thinking about your meditating on - all the time.

Only ego mind wants to sleep with other people, take it from a former sleeper.

Our enemies, politically, financially, interpersonally, socially, our ego-karma mind creates them all, and then blames them for it.

Ego desert mind is an addiction that doesn't exist.

Ego mind is a control freak.

"Be present as the watcher of your mind." *Eckhart Tolle*

Ego is a foreign country we've never been to, but want to go back to.

"I could not live in any of the worlds offered to me — the world of my parents, the world of war, the world of politics. I had to create a world of my own, like a climate, a country, an atmosphere in which I could breathe, reign, and recreate myself when destroyed by living. That, I believe, is the reason for every work of art." *Anaïs Nin From the kook: "The Diary of Anaïs Nin, 1947-1955"*

"Time is like a river made up of the events which happened, and a violent stream; for as soon as the thing has been seen, it is carried away, and another comes in its place, and this will be carried away too." *"Marcus Aurelius" translated by George Long.*

Do you think that the "little neighbor boy" in "The Ballad Of Frankie Lee And Judas Priest" was Frankie Lee's ego-karma mind "with his guilt so well concealed.?"

You know the question raised in the *Pete Seeger* song: "Where have all the flowers gone?" Equally important is asking, why have they come?

Desert ego mind is playing ping-pong for one, it's also playing pond-ping.

Unconditional love is free of all conditions.

Ego desert mind is a cult-urated.

Ego desert mind plays its game on the chessboard of our mind, knowing our every move before we make it, especially noticing when we want to stop playing.

Ego mind pulls the world apart pretending to pull it together, so it can pull it apart again.

A question we who have tried to go on a diet without success should ask ourselves is: What is eating us?

Ego mind always talks to itself no matter who it's talking to.

"We're on a karma mind hamster wheel, thinking someday we're gonna get there." *Karen Schooley*

Ego desert mind is looking for a cure for centuries of war, disease and poverty, hoping it is never found.

Over-eating is a way we can't get enough of something that has nothing to do with food.

Paranoia is an ego mental disorder that thinks it's normal.

Making all the lights doesn't necessarily mean you're going in the right direction.

How much longer in time will we spend, before *each* of us notice that we ego-karmic humans have created numberless centuries of systems: systems of nations, religious efforts, governments, laws, of weapons, etc., that have not only proved incapable of eliminating war, poverty, rich and poor, all internal and external conflict between people, but have repeatedly, without pause, enabled more of the same. When will we see the real problem: the separated ego mind that created the systems? We've deluded ourselves into thinking there are things like "culture wars," "relationship wars," cold wars,""economic wars," "political wars," etc. There is only one war of chaos going on: the ego-karma mind war, against itself. That is where peace negotiations must begin, until no longer needed.

"Do not be distracted from the coming of the Awareness." *Dalai Lama, from the movie "Kundun"*

In our lives we're taught how to choose everything, our careers, our friends, our food, our cars, our relationships, etc. But we are not taught how we can, that we can, choose our thoughts.

Ego-karma mind is the same as going out naked in -5° weather praying that you won't freeze to death.

If we knew who we really were, we wouldn't be here.

Button free mind is the meaning of love.

If we prevent others from making their own mistakes thinking we know what's best for them, unknowingly we admit their mistakes are our own.

Ego mind thought it left its source knowing it could not. This is the cause of all fear.

"The most beautiful people we have known are those who have known defeat, known suffering, known struggle, known loss, and have found their way out of the depths. These persons have an appreciation, a sensitivity, and an understanding of life that fills them with compassion, gentleness, and a deep loving concern. Beautiful people do not just happen." *Elisabeth Kübler-Ross*

"Judge tenderly of me." *Emily Dickinson*

"To forget is the secret of eternal youth. One grows old only through memory. There's much too little forgetting." *Erich Maria Remarque*

"When asked what he thought of Western civilization he said, 'I think it would be a good idea." *Mahatma Gandhi*

"Children are very wise intuitively; they know who loves them most, and who only pretends." *V.C. Andrews*

The ego takes no prisoners, it has them all.

Special spiritual gifts are not ours to keep, are just temporarily given.

Swami Satchidananda used to say, "If you're trying to find peace in your life the best thing to say is: e-go."

Human beings in general are fascinated by the concept of outer space. This fascination is an ego trick that we human beings have devised to prevent our selves from focusing on inner space.

"Like its politicians and its wars, society has the teenagers it deserves." *J.B. Priestley*

Finding one's spiritual path is like learning to play the piano. There are so many keys, so many chords, and so many possible many melodies. Play your way.

The outer world will begin to be a better place when enough of us realize there is no outer world.

With each thought destiny becomes *chosen* fate.

It is only personal demons we fight and argue with, there are no others.

My brother, my sister, myself, chose again.

Which came first, the chicken or the egg? Neither said the Awareness.

"In mornings dawning is evening begun. The moment is everything." *D. H. Lawrence*

No one will be free of poverty until all are free of poverty. If you need to ask how we can to do this, say for example, work harder, good job, education, know the right people, etc. you're asking the wrong question.

If each musician in a symphony orchestra played a different song at the same time, those listening would hear ego minds out of tune symphony simultaneously.

Good and bad are ego's way of having it both ways.

It is important to remember the early bird catches the worm, particularly if you like worms.

Love is the absence of conflict, of stress.

We are born into an ego world with an eye towards a future structured exactly like the past.

From time to time, depending on our readiness, Spiritual Mind may appear in a dream to remind us that we're just watching, that we're doing OK.

Words and language itself, are historically learned expressions of the objects they express. We have made them up, and believe in what we made. Words are symbols, symbols of symbols.

It is psychologically painful to recognize there is a difference between personal and universal love.

If it's true as Eastern spiritual psychology says, that there is no past or future, can there can be a time called now? And if there is no now, what time is it now?

Desert ego mind is Pandora's box and it is always open.

Ego pretends to see in the dark and after some time believes it can.

I heard through the grapevine that karma was nothing more than a rumor.

"Life in general has no meaning. Whatever meaning life has, must be assigned to it by the individual."
Alfred Alder

Sooner or later we will figure out that, there's nothing to figure out. And then we will have figured out all we need to know, about figuring things out.

The sheep herder herds sheep, allows the wool to grow, shaves it off to warm those cold, allowing it then to grow again. We could learn a lot from sheep.

Was there a reason "Hotel California" was on a dark desert highway?

Ego mind is a thera-pest.

The ego is one party rule with a self elected, house, senate, and president.

Desert ego-karma mind wants to be your beau-tox.

I heard a small child, maybe three, ask, "Mommie, what is a butterfly, where does it come from and why?" I wish I could have mommies answer, but couldn't because she whispered it in her child's ear.

A deep state runs the world: the karma unconscious mind.

"We are all soldiers of ego mind misfortune. Each moment brings us a chance to reverse that misfortune." *Reverend Rudra, formerly, Integral Yoga Institute, New York*

Ego loves a good fight because no matter who wins or loses, it wins.

People who need to dominant or control others have one personality trait in common: fear of themselves, and as a consequence, *all* others.

Ego is a flower pot minus flowers.

Ego desert mind is "The Pretender" in that Jackson Browne song.

"The challenge is in the moment; the time is always now." *James A. Baldwin*

Mi amiga, cuando alguien aprieta tu botón aprieta tu botón.

Most of the time we don't know we are at the end of our rope, until we realize we no longer have any rope.

Good and bad, winning and losing, are always relative. This is because they are one's individual perceptions, therefore they have no real meaning. Peace of mind is not relative, is not dependent on circumstances or perception. Peace is not relative. Peace Is.

"Meditation means creating a continual familiarity with a virtuous object in order to transform your mind." *Dalai Lama*

Ego is trickle down karma-nomics.

"There are very few friends that will lie down with you on empty streets in the middle of the night, without a word. No questions, no asking why, just quietly lay there with you, observing the stars, until you're ready to get back up on your feet again and walk the last bit home, softly holding your hand as a quiet way of saying "I'm here" *Charlotte Eriksson, Empty Roads & Broken Bottles: in search for The Great Perhaps*

Yin and Yang, male and female, are ego-karma split mind versions Spiritual Mind. If you didn't believe you were a split mind, could you have sex?

Why do we pay so called talented people millions of dollars, then applaud, and give them Academy Awards for something we do unconsciously each day?

"The soul becomes dyed with the color of its thoughts." *Marcus Aurelius*

Have you ever thought about the difference between karma sin buttons, and no karma sin buttons? And that, like good and bad, you can't have one, without having the other.

When you reach the top of ego desert mountain
you'll find you were always climbing down,
down, down, down,
under the sea, under the ground,
down and up, up and down.

I've come for you now
bearing karmic gifts,
speaks the ego dragon,
wearing his gilded crown.

it

we psychoanalyze it, over analyze it,
advertise it, brutalize it, exercise it,
we even idolize it!

what we don't do
is counterclockwise it, depersonalize it,
see it for what it is. but that's hard to do,
because it never is.

we even have given it
many different names,
so we can have lot's of
other someone's to blame.

it laughs in our face,
it knows we think it's real.
it even dares create courts of law
so it may hold itself accountable
for what it's never done.

let's go back to sleep now, turn out the light,
it's all going to be all right.
Good night. 😴

War And Conflict

What happens in the outer world, must occur first in the inner world, in the unconscious ego-karma mind.

All conflict is a reflection of personal inner war. We have to explain war as seen originating outside us, as a war in the outer world, so that we can avoid taking responsibility for it. Because of this, both sides blame the other for a war.

This truth can be seen by the casual use of the word "conflict," as a drugged, substitute word, for the word "war" in news reporting. What happens in the outer world, first must occur in the mind, in the unconscious ego-karma mind. We sugar coat this ego-karma, make it sweet to taste, easy to swallow . . . we call it: STRESS.

Not only that, but at the end of a button pushing, stress filled day at work, since *we have conditioned ourselves to accept stress as normal,* we reward ourselves for enduring it! We proudly congratulate ourselves for "doing a good job," we even unconsciously work over time, so we don't have to deal with the inner conflict we have created. *We condition ourselves to feel we need conflict to make us feel good about ourselves.*

External war, conflict, stress, call it what you like, are different versions of the same thing: a brutally cold, unloving, karmic inner war, upon our self.

I was standing off at the side,
   watching the people fight
over who was wrong, who was right,
   who won this, who won that.

And the people who used to be there;
   well, they aren't there anymore,
maybe some will never come back,
   those of us still here, can't be sure.

I'm a part of those old ones now, us 60s folks. So, they
don't ask us to fight in the outer war. Those of us still
around, we try to endure memories of empty faces,
empty faces of those whose lives had barely begun,
lifeless now except in our memory, in some wooden
box now, under some hard dirt ground now.

I knew, still know, some of those mothers and fathers,
they still find it hard to sleep, it never leaves them. So
they stay up late, drink, eat, get fat, get sick, watch
lot's of TV, (TV is their version of PTSD) dulling their
minds, so they don't have to think of it all the time.

What happens in the outer world, <u>must occur first in
the inner world,</u> in the unconscious ego-karma mind.

-

Victims And Victimizers

Ego mind recognizes, but is afraid to face, the meaninglessness, the emptiness, of its conflicted existence. An existence empty of love, empty of Spiritual Mind.

So it avoids taking responsibility for its own emptiness by blaming others for it, by creating karmic enemies to blame, which is a form of self hate, an insecurity in it self which it does not want to see, and so must project into the empty faces of all so called others, even those it pretends to love, for it is incapable of love.

To free itself of its own self created unconscious karmic emptiness, *caused by ego minds necessary belief in time,* it must always find someone else to blame for its misery. So seeing itself as a victim of circumstances outside itself, it seeks victimizer's.

"Isn't he's a little bit, like you and me."

From the Beatles song "Nowhere Man,"

How Karma And Time Never Happened

There is a place where time never began, John gave it his name, "Strawberry Fields Forever," "nothing is real, nothing to get hung about."

The thought of both karma and time began at the same instant when the thought of separation from Spiritual Mind - which cannot be done - occurred. However, since we have free will to think whatever we want, it can be imagined.

At that same instant, the thought that it was possible to leave Spiritual Mind, two seemingly separated, seemingly real forms, male and female, Yin and Yang, occurred.

From those two thoughts, evolved all cause and effect thoughts, *all* thoughts of past and future, all thoughts of ego, of karma, of individual existence taking place in time. And of all of us, as separate from each other.

The Apple

In a way, all the Beatles wrote all the songs, one may have contributed more to one song than the other, but there was only one Apple in the Beatle's song satchel.

"We were half a million strong
And everywhere were
the songs and the celebration

And I dreamed I saw the bomber jet planes
Riding shotgun in the sky
Turning into butterflies above our nation

We are stardust, we are golden
We are billionear-old carbon
And we've got to get ourselves
back to the garden

We are stardust, we are golden
We are caught up in the devils bargain
And we've got to get ourselves
back to the garden"
From the song "Woodstock" by Joni Mitchell

- Swami Satchidananda Introducing the Woodstock Festival -

"All Things Must Pass"

It's worth considering, as some have, after George
Harrison released his first solo album after the Beatles
break-up, "All Things Must Pass," that Barry
Feinstein's album cover art, with the photograph
showing George bordered by four gnomes, along with
the album title, could be interpreted as a declaration of
departure from George's days as a "Fab Four" Beatle,
and as a start, as an artist, and spiritual life, of his own.

So, since the George we all knew
"All Those Years Ago"
is now, materially incommunicado,
shouldn't we consider that;
our life experiences should be seen
as a loving re-minder class,
a reminder, re-finder class in,
"All Things Must Pass."

"Thoroughly unprepared, we take the step into the
afternoon of life. Worse still, we take this step with the
false presumption that our truths and our ideals will
serve us as hitherto." *Carl Jung.*

When I Saw Susan Today

When I saw Susan today
I remembered her face the moment she said:

"Please always remember me this way."

She didn't remember me today,
Susan didn't know who I was,
although she smiled at me,
she didn't remember.

So I just took a deep breath someway,
closed my eyes, and tried,
tried to remember her, yes tried to remember her,
remember her as she was on that day,

on that day before dementia had its way.

That was the last day I heard Susan say;
"Please always remember me this way."

Sister Beautiful

I have a sister beautiful,
I am so glad to know her:
Absence is not her way.

Oh sister beautiful,
Each verse of your sweetness
comes to me of its own.

Oh sister beautiful,
I glimpse thee in all I do,
and thus with clearer eyes
Do I see both myself and you.

Oh, sister beautiful,
How many ways may I call your name?

I have a sister beautiful,
I am so glad to know you:
Absence is not your way.

Farewell Those Loved

Farewell those loved, those gone away,
those no longer to be found, those no longer
to be seen.

Farewell those broken,
those devotions no longer embrace,
those ego-karmic time renders, forgotten,

Farewell those loved,
those come greet us tender,
those come confess the sword.

Fare-thee-well then,
all those those loved.

Clear Light

Ages of Ice,
Ages of Warmth,
can chosen to be perceived right,
with the arriving of the awareness,
the awareness of the
Clear Light.

Clear Light,
Yin and Yang, Yang and Yin.

So when observing with Ages eyesight,
we should endeavor to choose Clear Light.

SOMEDAY YOU'RE JUST   GONNA' FADE AWAY,
SOMEDAY YOU'RE JUST GONNA' FADE AWAY.
SOMEDAY WHEN YOU MAY LEAST EXPECT IT,
YOU'RE NOT GOING TO BE HERE TODAY.

SO EITHER WAY,
DON'T WAIT UNTIL SOMEDAY
WHEN YOU MAY LEAST EXPECT IT,
YOU GOTTA' START TODAY,
START TODAY TO DIRECT IT.

[SOMEDAY WHEN YOU MAY LEAST EXPECT IT,
YOU AIN'T GONNA' BE YOUNG ANYMORE.

THIS WAY, THAT WAY, ONE WAY OR THE OTHER,
YOU AIN'T GONNA' BE OLD ANYMORE.]

WHERE DID IT ALL GO?
WHEN DID I GET THIS WAY?
YOU CAN'T PREDICT THE FUTURE,
BUT YOU CAN START TO DIRECT IT.

SOMEDAY WHEN YOU MAY LEAST EXPECT IT,
YOU'RE JUST GONNA FADE AWAY.
SOMEDAY YOU'RE JUST NOT
GOING TO BE HERE TODAY.

Miracle Run

With heart's remembrance well earned,
with devotion's willingness steadfast,
someday these well used ancient shoes
shall we, at the exit, surrender.

Spiritual Memory will greet us then,
once again, as once again before.
Strangers then, shall we be no more,
beside you here, beside you near,
beside you dear, at Miracle Run.

Besides you here at weepings end,
at pathways meet, at pathways vanish,
at pathways need undone.

I'm beside myself when
I'm not beside you there,
*"Da Doo Ron Ron,
Da Doo Ron Ron."

Beside you there,
my dearest one,
beside you there,
at Miracle Run.

*From the Crystals Song, "Da Doo Ron Ron"

*The Sea That Brings All Chances

Is it not time at last, and time at last forevermore,
To leave our home as we have before,
To set sail, with steadfast devotion,
Our sturdy boat to sea?

Is it not time at last, and time at last forevermore,
To befriend our heart, our un-watched noble heart,
and to slowly start our sturdy boat
toward mysteries foreign shore?

Is it not time at last, and time at last forevermore,
To make not but gradual advances,
But rather to sail with boldness and doubt:
On the sea that brings all chances.

And yes, oh yes, to un-voice the dances's,
no matter what may seem the chances,
Giving thankful remembrance
to those courageous gone before,
gone before, on the sea that brings all chances!

For are we not mere passing personal glances
on the sea that brings all chances?
Are we not that Holy Mist devoted sweetheart of yore?

Therefore, let us entrust all advances,
as a chance to choose anew once more,
on the sea that brings all chances.

*Title from "Tristan and Isolde," by Thomas Gottfried

Relationships - Breaking Up, Making Up

Make a Spirirtual Mind effort to understand how this making up or breaking up occurred. Consider that unconsciously, *through your past ego-karma identity,* you chose it to be this way. Ask yourself (and/or talk about it with someone you know who cares) why you chose this relationship at this time. You can both try to, very gently, ask yourself, and perhaps ask each other, what past karma you each brought to this relationship, to this make up or break up. If you can't understand how it happened, it will happen again.

If you do break up, without blame as best you can, say you're sorry, but you did the best you could at the time. Don't hold back the tears.

Photo © Todd Weinstein

"Once a story's told
It can't help but grow old
Roses do
Lovers too, so cast
Your seasons to the wind
And hold me, dear
Oh, hold me, dear"
From the song, "Were All Alone," Rita Coolidge

Working With All Everyday Life Issues

As I quoted Virginia Wolf on page 6, "You cannot find peace by avoiding life," so being realistic, while we think we live in this karmic world, there are decisions, choices, to be make, and we must make them, no matter how things turn out, no matter if we think we are making them with Button mind or Spiritual Mind. We can't understand what we are not ready to understand. Something's can take a while to work out.

It can be very difficult, I speak for myself as well, to comprehend that "to ask our spiritual guide for the answer - *is the answer*," to all everyday problems. This is because, no matter what we think the problem is, there is only one problem, and so only one answer. The Answer is to recall: We are spiritual beings having a human experience. Each time we choose to recall our True nature, in that instant, we are there Now.

Press Karma Delete

We have a karma delete button we can press *at anytime,* not only when something pushes our ego-karma button. It is a short spiritual phrase, in the Eastern spiritual approach, it's called, a mantra, but call it whatever you like. The way it works is: You chose a phrase, any phrase you like. When you repeat it, it helps you remember, you're spiritual being having human experience. *"*Make it short, 1, 2, 3, 4 words."* Use your ego-karma delete button, it is a way of *consciously choosing* to see with spiritual vision.
*Swami Satchidananda

And, it's easy to use, to do, because, you can repeat it, press it, anywhere, anytime, at work, while shopping, going somewhere, etc., And don't worry if you forget, after a while, if you repeat it often enough, it will become a habit, and like any habit, you'll do it without even knowing, Spiritual Mind will just take right over.

Or, you can use any of the quotes and sayings in this book, they can help us remember how we want to experience our lives. They can be memorized, underlined, *used as affirmations* as I said earlier, to delete karma. Carry this book, or others like it, around with you, keep it by your bed, or on your living room table, in your car, you know what I mean, to turn to anytime. Spend time with it, like a loving friend, use it as a re-minder regarding the value of again and again, *consciously choosing* to make the right choice.

Use The **SUV/GPS** Watcher/Chooser Mind

The Watcher/Chooser is the **G**uidance **P**eace **S**ystem, the **K**arma **D**elete mind, *the closet thought to Now, to this instant, to the Awareness, that we can conceive of.*

It works just like our car GPS, which takes us where we need to go in the outer physical world. But, in both the outer and inner world's, *we must consciously choose* to set it where we want to go.

The more often we to choose to use the Watcher/ Chooser Mind GPS, the more we make it a habit, like any habit, it takes over, and takes us where we want to go, without our even knowing it. You know, it's like listening to a song we love over and over, all of a sudden we just know the words. It's like we didn't even have to try to, it just happens on its own.

Every time we choose to see with Watcher/Chooser Mind, the more we just Observe/Watch, what we are seeing, with our Spiritual Mind, or our spiritual guide, or whatever name we chose to give That presence. And so, the more we free ourselves of our *past* karmic bag of thoughts, of history's accumulated/habituated thoughts of stress, regret, disappointment, depression, war, fear, sin, guilt, self doubt, anger, and all the rest of the ego-karma minds nonexistent list of directives, of thoughts - all seeming different, but all just different versions of the same thing - the past. There is no past; except for the memory meaning we have given it.

283

"Watching - Choosing"
The Way, The Benefits

Dear reader,
As we choose our own way to watch karmic mind,
and choose to love those we see with Spiritual Mind,
from those closest, to those we seem not to know;
let us gently do our best to recall the words of
"Instant Karma," and that there are no accidents,
and those of George's song, "Who Can See It,"

"My life belongs to me
My love belongs to who can see it"

"Karma is the set of circumstances that you have chosen to inhabit in this lifetime in order to find the areas, not yet in truth." *Emmanuel's Book, book one*

"Life will give you whatever experience that is most helpful for the evolution of your consciousness. How do you know this is the experience you need? Because this is the experience you are having at the moment." *Eckhart Tolle*

"You cannot control the behavior of others, but you can always choose how you respond to it." *Roy T. Bennett*

"I believe that we are solely responsible for our choices, and we have to accept the consequences of every deed, word, and thought throughout our lifetime." *Elisabeth Kubler-Ross*

"Evaluating the benefits and drawbacks of any relationship is your responsibility. You do not have to passively accept what is brought to you. You can choose." *Deborah Day*

It pretends otherwise, but karmic mind is afraid to love. We can practice, learn, choose, to see differently.

"Choose once again is still your only hope." *Helen Schucman*

"The developing personality obeys, no caprice, no command, no insight, only brute necessity, it needs the motivating force of inner or outer fatalities." *Carl Jung*

"Our lives are a sum total of the choices we have made." *Wayne Dyer*

"What you choose also chooses you." *Kamand Kojouri*

"We are the thoughts we choose to keep." *A.D. Posey*

> *"This is for all the lonely people*
> *Thinking that life has passed them by*
> *Don't give up until you drink from the silver cup*
> *And ride that highway in the sky"*
> From the song, "Lonely People," America

"Choice is the basis of every part of your existence, but so is fear. The difference is, choice creates movement, where fear limits movement." *Réné Gaudette*

"To choose or not to choose, is still a choice for which you alone are responsible." *Gary Cox,*

"Life is a matter of choices, and every choice you make makes you." *John C. Maxwell*

"The most difficult thing is the decision to act, the rest is merely tenacity. The fears are paper tigers. You can do anything you decide to do. You can act to change and control your life; and the procedure, the process is its own reward." *Amelia Earhart*

"Beliefs are choices. First you choose your beliefs. Then your beliefs affect your choices." *Roy T. Bennett*

"We are our choices." *Jean-Paul Sartre*

"In a choice between love and fear, choose love." *Marianne Williamson*

"One cannot choose wisely for a life unless he dares to listen to himself, his own self, at each moment of his life." *Abraham Maslow*

"Our task must be to free ourselves, by widening our circle of compassion to embrace all living creatures and the whole of nature and its beauty." *Albert Einstein*

"We are here to awaken from our illusion of separateness." *Thich Naht Hanh*

"No matter what the situation is, re-mind yourself, I have a choice. You and I are essentially infinite choice-makers. In every moment of our existence, we are in that field of all possibilities where we have access to an infinity of choices." *Deepak Chopra*

When something pushes your button remember, "Trials are but lessons that you failed to learn presented once again, so where you made a faulty choice before you now can make a better one, and thus escape all pain that what you chose before has brought to you." *A Course In Miracles*

When something pushes your button remember what Yogi Bhajan said: "If you are willing to look at another's behavior towards you as a reflection of the state of their relationship with themselves rather than a statement about your value as a person, then you will, over a period of time, cease to react at all."

When something pushes your button, Choose with Watcher Mind to remember what Don Miguel Ruiz said: "Don't take anything personally: *Nothing others do is because of you.* What others say and do is a projection of their own reality, their own dream. When you are immune to the opinions and actions of others, you won't be the victim of needless suffering."

When something pushes your button remember: "Whether describing a king, an assassin, a thief, an honest man, a prostitute, a nun, a young girl, or a stall-holder in a market, it is always ourselves we are describing." *Guy de Maupassant*

"The only way of knowing a person is to love them without hope." *Walter Benjamin*

-

Choosing to see with Spiritual Mind presupposes
a belief in inter-dependent, peaceful origination.

One way or the other, choosing is continuous.

In our lives we are taught to choose everything we do,
why not our thoughts?

Why not find, try to find a way, your way,
to think about all this kind of stuff each day?
Maybe when getting up, or before going to sleep,
or at any time you find yourself knee-deep.

Larry Kane, The Beatles, Who Is Padman?

Dear reader, I would like to tell you about my friend Larry. We're oldies but goodies, friends for over 60 years! You can read about Larry, his life's work, his karmic relationship to the Beatles, on the next page.

The Beatles, Scott Regen, back stage, Sunday, August 13, 1966, Olympia Stadium, Detroit. Photo by my 'gone now' friend, Bob.

Who Is Padman?

If karmically I wasn't a DJ in the 60s era named Scott Regen, on WKNR, Detroit, listening over and over to those Beatle spiritual and social commentary songs, and those of other artists - just like so many of us did - I would not be the me I am today; that is to say, my now "**a**lso **k**nown **a**s" spiritual name, Padman.

This echoes a name change 60's time. It was when the Beatles became "Sergeant Pepper's Lonely Hearts Club Band." And, Scott Regen/Padman wouldn't have met the Beatles, if it wasn't for my friend Larry, who I first met in 1961. What goes around comes around.

About Larry

Larry can tell you things about the Beatles no one else can, all from "first hand experience."

He was with them "face to face," interviewing them on every stop of all their American tours. The interviews were then broadcast to over 50 radio stations across America. Larry has the largest collection of personal interviews with the Beatles in the world. For more on Larry and his book, Google Larry Kane's, "Ticket To Ride." The book includes a CD with his Beatle interviews. The book has a foreword by Dick Clark. It was a New York Times, Los Angeles Times bestseller.

Larry had a major part in Ron Howard's film "Eight Days A Week," was an honored guest September 15, 2016 in London at the film's premier alongside Ron Howard, Paul McCartney and Ringo Starr, and also helped behind the scenes with the Beatles "Get Back." Along with other books on the Beatles he wrote, Larry is an Emmy Award-winning newsman. He spent 36 years as a Philadelphia news anchor, retired in 2002, and is now a special contributor for KYW Newsradio.

Writing This Book

The majority of stuff in this book was written two, three, four in the morning, when I'd wake up, and thoughts would just start coming. When it first began happening I thought I had to just go back to sleep, because I needed a good nights rest. But then I would write one thing or another, and then finally just decide to sit up in bed and see what my mind, or whatever it was, had to say, and then when it was done dictating, I'd go back to sleep.

You know it's hard to explain this in a way, I can't explain how I came to write this book. You would never think someone like me would do that with my background, the way I started out in life, I mean you'll understand if it happens to you, otherwise there's really no need, well maybe some need if someone mentions it to you, but otherwise I don't think so.

I was thinking I had finished writing this book many times, but thoughts just kept coming. I think it's like people like J.D.Salinger. He never could've predicted all that stuff that happened to him in his life, like naming his book "Catcher in the Rye," like the war, P.T.S.D, all that stuff, having kids, marriage, his life turning out the way it did. What do you make of it all?

You know what I think it was? It was that Holden Caulfield wanted to try to catch all of us kids before we fell off, and he did it by trying to catch his.

I was teaching at Rollins College, and one day during a class discussion, a women, her name is Valli, she summed up what I didn't know I needed to know: "We are Spiritual beings having a human experience." And so, memory of ego-karma will gradually fade away, drift away, nothing of it all, shall we recall.

I'm writing all this because I've been ego partner to thoughts and acts (anger, guilt, fear, stress, lying, self doubt, self indulgence, etc.) which have undermined Chardin's belief. I've concluded the feelings and actions that flowed from those ego-karma thoughts could not change the Created origin of my Being.

So, finding a way to become *consciously* aware "We are all Spiritual beings having a human experience," gradually has grown to be my life's purpose.

I encourage awareness of this purpose through everyday life experiences, as often (without regret when I forget) as comfortably possible. I pursue this effort by being responsive to Carl Jung's truism, "Knowing your darkness, is the best method for dealing with the darknesses of other people."

I feel optimistic, that sooner or later, each of you reading this book - which you couldn't be reading by accident, because karma, also known as cause and effect, is infallible - will find some thoughts that speak directly to your Original heart, in your search for your spiritual unfolding, so that you can find a way - *your way* - of knowing what to do when encountering, and identifying, your ego-karma buttons in the *"everyday practical problems of life,"* and letting them go, and in that very process, remembering: your problems have already been solved, because you never had any,

So, let us each do our part, so the button ego-karma mind system will not continue to be an unconscious threat to the worlds physical and psychological well being, comparable to meeting a Mapogo lion, some late afternoon, on some dark deserted road of the Sabi Sands Game Reserve, stopping, smiling, and saying: Hello, it's nice to meet you.
*Padman 🙏

*Padman means Lotus

293

There are no buttons

"Imagine"

In the sixties the Beatles brought Eastern spiritual thinking to the Western world through their music. T*he feeling of the 60s, the meaning of the 60s,* peace, love, and harmony between all people, still lives in all hearts, those of us who were there, and those of us who weren't. Yes, there were things that happened back then that weren't so beautiful, and we can't make believe they never happened. I stood across the street from Motown on Grand Boulevard in Detroit after police said it was OK for us to go back on the street after the heartbreaking 12th St. riots, so I'm no bliss ninny. Those here now, it is we who must nurture the peace and love message of the spiritual 60s living in all hearts.

The words and feelings of John Lennons "Imagine," the meaning of the Imagine Mandela, Central Park across from the Dakota, 79th/CPW, where John and Yoko lived with their son Sean, near Bow Bridge where they would walk, need to be *consciously called to mind* in a way right for us. We can *choose to free our karma history.*

We can fine a way to *choose* to "Imagine."

"Spiritual life really begins in earnest when the seeker starts to awaken to the unsettling fact that the ego-karma mind's very approach to finding happiness is what is disturbing the happiness."
Swami Asokananda, President,
Integral Yoga Institute, New York

Epilogue

Many books say the same things as this one. Read as many books as you can, watch stuff on line, go to lots of classes, find the right spiritual path for you. As I said earlier, the right method for the wrong person, is the wrong method. Don't give up until glimpsing the fact that, regardless of circumstances, we can only experience our lives in one or two ways, with or without peace of mind. Within the effort itself, is the loving understanding that "You are a spiritual being, 'thinking" you are having a human experience."

"About Padman"

I've had a spiritual advising practice since 2002. My personal journey began in 1971 when I experienced what some say Mark Twain said: "A man who carries a cat by the tail learns something he can learn in no other way."

I taught classes at Integral Yoga Institute, New York, for about 15 years, and was certified there to teach meditation in 2002. All classes I taught were inter-faith, and about "making everyday practical use" of Eastern spiritual psychology and philosophy.

I taught at Rollins College, Winter Park, Florida, an Orlando suburb, for around 6 years, as part of their "Center For Life Long Learning Program." The name Rollins gave those classes is what I teach: Life Long Learning. I also taught primarily at Red Sun Yoga, Winter Springs, Florida, also an Orlando suburb, for around 10 years. If you have any thoughts or questions: egobutton@gmail.com Namaste

Give to those at 335 E. 145th Street,
Bronx, New York, 10451.
The Third Avenue bus, the # 6 train,
postal mail, or just plain walking
will get it there. They care.

Made in United States
Orlando, FL
05 December 2024

54461372R00178